# He Touched Me

# He Touched Me

Rex Trogdon

HE TOUCHED ME
By: Rex Trogdon
Copyright © 2011
GOSPEL FOLIO PRESS
All Rights Reserved

Published by
GOSPEL FOLIO PRESS
304 Killaly St. W.
Port Colborne, ON L3K 6A6
CANADA

ISBN: 9781897117880

Cover design by Lisa Martin

All Scripture quotations from the
King James Version unless otherwise noted.

Printed in USA

# Dedication

Dedicated to my wife, my beloved Nance, my helper and my very best friend.

You have touched my life in a most wonderful way. Your love and encouragement means more to me than I could ever express with pen and ink. Being "heirs together in the grace of life," we know that the best is yet to come.

# Special Heartfelt Thanks

Nancy joins me in sending our heartfelt thanks to my brother, Alan Trogdon, our dear friend, Bonnie Williams, and our neighbor, Carol Burrows, for their work in editing and advising me in this writing project, *He Touched Me.* Your time invested, patience and kindness in corrections is greatly valued and appreciated. May the Lord bless you greatly in return.

Our love and thanks to our fellow saints at Believers Bible Chapel who encourage us in the Lord's service and always overwhelm us in the love of God through our Lord. What a happy fellowship we enjoy in Christ! May we continue to see His hand upon us as we stand together with both feet upon the reminder, *"Without Me you can do nothing,"* and upon the promise, *"I can do all things through Christ who strengthens me."*

Gratefully in Christ,
Rex & Nancy Trogdon

# Table of Contents

# He Touched Me!

He touched me, O He touched me,
And O the joy that floods my soul!
Something happened, and now I know,
He touched me and made me whole.

Shackled by a heavy burden,
'Neath a load of guilt and shame,
Then the hand of Jesus touched me,
And now I am no longer the same.

He touched me, O He touched me,
And O the joy that floods my soul!
Something happened, and now I know,
He touched me and made me whole.

Since I met this Blessed Saviour,
Since He cleansed and made me whole,
I will never cease to praise Him;
I'll shout it while eternity rolls.

He touched me, O He touched me,
And O the joy that floods my soul!
Something happened, and now I know,
He touched me and made me whole.

—Bill Gaither

# Foreword

"For we have not an high priest which cannot be touched with the feeling of our infirmities; but was in all points tempted like as we are, yet without sin." —Hebrews 4:15

While on earth, the Lord Jesus, reaching out to man or multitude, responded with a touch to the point of need. His earthly ministry was one of caring and sharing as He sympathized with people like us. He was moved with compassion then, and He still is today.

Our great High Priest is *"able to save to the uttermost"* because *"He ever lives to make intercession"* for us. *"Touched with the feeling of our infirmities,"* He knows what affects our lives. Therefore, being touched by what touches us, He is affected.

This book is offered with a fourfold purpose.

First, it is intended to bring the **Scriptures** before us. God has promised that His Word will not return to Him void but will accomplish the purpose for which it is sent. Take the time to read each portion of Scripture that has been placed at the beginning of each chapter for your convenience and learning.

Secondly, it is to tell the **story**, relived using some sanctified imagination. A story communicates truth in every day living and is one of the clearest ways of teaching.

Thirdly, it gives an opportunity to **study**. The events of the Scripture are woven together with truths that are teachable in outline form. Use the outlines to share in your ministry to others or to ponder the points in an orderly fashion.

Lastly, it is a **sermon**. It seeks to provide truth in a multi-level presentation so that it can be applied to our lives. The truth sets us free to live according to it. May these exhortations be an encouragement to better know the Lord. As the prophet Hosea says, *"Let us know; let us pursue the knowledge of the Lord"* (Hosea 6:3).

Overall, this book is presented with the desire to glorify the Lord Jesus Christ. You and I have the privilege of being a magnifying glass that others might see Him better through us. Why? Because we can all claim, **"He touched me!"**

# Strength to Serve

## The Scriptures

"So He touched her hand, and the fever left her. And she arose and served them." —Matthew 8:15

The Bible says, that by the mouth of two or three witnesses every fact may be confirmed. We have more than just witnesses confirming the facts of the Bible. We have three men who either lived these events firsthand or made careful investigation and interviewed the people who were involved so as to give us an accurate account. Therefore, I like to notice the full picture that the synoptic Gospels of Matthew, Mark, and Luke give of the events that took place in the life and ministry of the Lord Jesus.

Take the time to read these few verses that tell the same story as seen through three different sets of eyes and that are told from different perspectives. After we look at the story we will take the time to distinguish and learn from each one.

*"Now when Jesus had come into Peter's house, He saw his wife's mother lying sick with a fever.*

*"So He touched her hand, and the fever left her. And she arose and served them."* —Matthew 8:14-15

*"Now as soon as they had come out of the synagogue, they entered the house of Simon and Andrew, with James and John.*

*"But Simon's wife's mother lay sick with a fever, and they told Him*

*about her at once.*

*"So He came and took her by the hand and lifted her up, and immediately the fever left her. And she served them."* —Mark 1:29-31

*"Now He arose from the synagogue and entered Simon's house. But Simon's wife's mother was sick with a high fever, and they made request of Him concerning her.*

*"So He stood over her and rebuked the fever, and it left her. And immediately she arose and served them."* —Luke 4:38-39

# The Story

"No time to spare," Simon's mother-in-law said to herself. Everything was set. So much had happened in the last year that she was just glad to be settled again and living with her daughter and her family. She was thankful to do what she knew best — entertain dinner guests.

"Feed them," she thought; that's the way she made folks happy in her home. She toyed with the idea of changing her menu, but, no, she would stick to the dish that she knew best. It had to be the best. Her daughter's husband and his fishing partners were coming to dinner. Today would be a day to be remembered with all her family and the special guest, the preacher from Nazareth. He had offered a new opportunity to her son-in-law, Simon.

"Nazareth," she breathed with contempt. "Twenty-five miles away is not far enough. What a place! The synagogue is still reeling, no doubt, from what took place there last week. You would think they would be glad to have one of their own do so well in ministry.

"I would give anything to have been there when He read from the scroll just to see their mouths drop open in amazement as He kept telling them, 'Today this Scripture is fulfilled!' They said the silence was deafening! Then followed the murmurs, the questions, the reaction, and His challenge, "You will surely quote the proverb, 'Physician, heal yourself!'"

"I cannot believe He would then bring up Elijah and Elisha and their ministry to the Zarephath widow and Naaman, the Syrian! Yes, I would love to have been a fly on the wall. On second thought, no, I would not. That kind of stuff really bothers me. I like the quiet life here on the lake with my family.

"Well, I had better get on with this quiet life. The Sabbath is close.

"How did He just walk through them at that steep cliff? I hope someone asks Him at dinner. I must remember to ask Andrew to bring it up."

15

Just then, walking up the path, she felt tired, dizzy. "Oh, please, no," she thought to herself. "Not today! This is no time to be sick. I must lie down. 'Help me, Lord, to shake this and quick.' At least everything is prepared. They'll do fine without me. Maybe I will quote the proverb to Him, *'Physician, heal Yourself,'* **and me too.**"

The Lord was glad to be in Capernaum again, a place blessed with good fishing and fertile hills. The synagogue was different than in Nazareth, even the building itself, newly constructed by the centurion stationed there. Moreover, these people by the sea needed Him more than they even knew.

Yes, it was good to be back in Capernaum, the new home base for His ministry in Galilee. What miracles He had already performed there and how well they had responded to His ministry! However, with light comes responsibility, and this city together with two other cities of the triad, Bethsaida and Chorazin, would be given much light.

Andrew spoke with some of the people who gathered outside his house. He related the events of the day concerning Jesus but started by sharing his own experience of meeting Him. "Since the day John the Baptist encouraged John and me to follow Him, I knew He was like no one I had met before. I was fully convinced that this was the Messiah. He was the One that Simon and I spoke of as young boys growing up. We dreamed of this day, and here it is, in our lifetime. I remember that I could hardly contain myself when I saw Simon and blurted out, 'We've found Him —the Messiah!' The rest is more than history. It has become **my-story.**"

He then went on to tell them how glad he was about the Messiah's decision to move to Capernaum. "Today, at the synagogue, the Lord Jesus spoke with such authority that the effect was felt by all. All who listened were astonished at His teaching. Their response was, 'What powerful words!' but it wasn't only how He spoke, it was what He did. It was amazing!

"While the Messiah was reading from the Torah and giving

the sense of its meaning, we were all sitting and listening intently, hanging onto His every word. Suddenly, someone shoved me from behind as if he were running at full speed and collided with me. I turned to see the man as he pushed his way toward the front of the synagogue. The voice was loud and unforgettable that came from the man who was obviously engulfed with a presence of evil. He was pleading, 'Let us alone!' He began spewing out the words over and over, 'What have we to do with You, Jesus of Nazareth?' His face contorted in horror as he cried, 'Did You come to destroy us? I know You, who You are — the Holy One of God!'"

"Wow!" Andrew interjected. "What an introduction for the Messiah to the Capernaum synagogue! We were all backing up, cowering. Jesus was the only One still standing. He spoke again without fear and demanded, 'Be quiet and come out of him!'

"It was as if the man was flung from the balcony as he fell in the midst of the synagogue. He was so listless that we thought he was dead. Then he stretched out his fingers, bent back his shoulders, and lifted himself from the floor. He sat straight up, and we gasped. As he rose to his feet, we were amazed. He was unscathed. I mean, not even a mark on him.

"As we spoke in hushed tones among ourselves about what had just happened, someone called out, 'Even the unclean spirits obey Him!' We broke into cheers that reverberated throughout the stones of the building. We could hardly wait to spread the news. A crowd was gathering.

"There was so much excitement that we all stood around after it was over, but that's not all that happened," Andrew paused. "Then I remembered that I was to bring Jesus home from the synagogue. Just inside the door of his house, Simon met us and explained to Jesus about his mother-in-law's sudden illness and wondered if He could help her. About that time Simon's wife came from her room and cried, 'Please, come quickly!' Jesus followed them into the room. He entered with that same boldness we saw earlier at the synagogue. He stood over her and rebuked the fever. It left just like the demons left that poor man! Then with a gentle touch on her hand, He lifted her up.

"She got right up. Her eyes filled with tears of joy, and she left the room immediately. We heard the clamour among the women as she worked her way among the others who were already starting to put the food on the table. So excited, thrilled that she got to serve the meal she had prepared for Him and her other guests. His touch was all she needed." Andrew turned to address the entire crowd that had gathered at Simon's door and raised his voice so that all could hear, "He's all that any of us need!"

# The Study

I. STRENGTH FOR SERVICE (Matt. 8:14-15; Mark 1:29-31; Luke 4:38-39)

   A. The Setting

      1. Place—At Simon Peter's house in Capernaum (Matt. 8:14)

         a. Peter and his wife lived there

         b. Andrew lived with them (Mark 1:29)

         c. James and John came for a visit, too (Mark 1:29)

      2. Time - On a Sabbath Day (Mark 1:21)

   &#10551; This is the second of the seven Sabbath miracles of our Lord

         a. First, Meeting (Mark 1:21)

            1) His words—The Lord had taught in the synagogue

            2) His works—He cast out a demon (Mark 1:21)

         b. Then, eating (Mark 1:29; 4:38) - The Lord went from the synagogue to Peter's house for a meal

   B. Her Sickness

      1. Her Condition

         a. She was lying sick with a fever (Matt. 8:14c)

         b. Luke, being a doctor, tells us that it was a *high fever* (Luke 4:38)

            1) No doubt, dizzy and weak

            2) The indication of fighting an infection

         c. They report her condition to the Lord (Mark 1:30; Luke 4:38)

            1) Urgent Care—*They told the Lord about her at once* (Mark 1:30)

19

  2) Appointment—*They made a request concerning he*r (Luke 4:38)

  3) "The Doctor will *see* you now" — *"He saw his wife's mother"* (Matt. 8:14)

2. Her Cure

 a. Dr. Luke gives a dramatic description of the Lord's power over disease (Luke 4:39)

  1) *He stood over her*—The Greek uses a phrase that presents the Lord as One who *stands* by, in charge and defends by assault

  2) He *rebuked the fever, and it left her*

 b. Mark expresses His help (Mark 1:31)

  1) He *came*

  2) He *took her by the hand*

  3) He *lifted her up and immediately the fever left her*

&#10087; He *lifted* her up – That is what James 5:15 says, *"And the Lord will raise him up."*

 c. Matthew emphasizes His *touch* (Matt. 8:15)

  1) The cause—*So He touched her hand*

  2) The effect—*She arose and served them*

C. Her Service—*She arose and served them* (Matt. 8:15; Mark 1:31; Luke 4:39)

&#10087; He touched her hand, and it made the difference. It was, as one contemporary songwriter puts it, "the touch of the Master's hand."

# The Sermon

I like to notice how Matthew, Mark, and Luke, the synoptic Gospels, give us the full picture of the events that took place in the life of the Lord Jesus.

The setting was in Capernaum. Capernaum = kafer nahum, the village of comfort. It was the new home base for the Lord's ministry after they drove Him to the edge of a cliff in Nazareth. Nazareth was known as a place of debauchery and crime, a place that merchants stopped for the night on their way to Jerusalem to sell their wares. It is no wonder that Nathanael quizzically responded to Philip's good news, *"We have found the Messiah ... Jesus of Nazareth,"* saying, *"Can any good come out of Nazareth?"*

Philip gave the right response, *"Come and see."* We can surely take a lesson from Philip when inviting people to the Saviour. Just come and see if the Lord Jesus is not all He claims to be.

It is hard to believe that Nazareth rejected the only One who could have improved its reputation, but it did. The Lord then moved to Capernaum on the Sea of Galilee where He spent the better part of His three years of public ministry. We would naturally have thought the Lord would be born and live in Jerusalem. Not so, said the prophets. He would be born in Bethlehem and live in Galilee. *"Those who sit in darkness shall see light."* How much the people of Galilee saw and were responsible for (Matt. 4:13-16)!

Capernaum was the location where a number of miracles were performed by the Lord Jesus. The healing of Peter's mother-in-law was the second recorded miracle that took place there. Also in Capernaum a centurion was stationed who showed kindness in building a synagogue for the community. He, too, received a miracle and an honourable mention by the Lord for his great faith.

Moving from the synagogue scene, although it was quite an experience that none would forget, the Lord made His way to the home of Simon Peter. Things were in disarray as you can imagine with the mother of the house lying sick with a fever. Many times we too struggle when our best-laid plans don't go accordingly. In this time of confusion, Simon Peter's family began to call on the Lord for help.

I think about our medical facilities today and the way we are just like the people in the story. Follow through the differing accounts and imagine yourself in the story...

Luke, being a doctor, takes the orderly route as if to make an appointment at his office, *"They made a* **request** *concerning her"* (Luke 4:39). Can't you picture your own experience when you need help but must go through the proper procedure only to find that the doctor's schedule is full for the next two months? How good to know the Great Physician always has time to see you.

Mark, on the other hand, represents the people who storm the gates of the Urgent Care facility whose red neon light glows in the night sky. *"...and they told Him about her* **at once"** (Mark 1:30). There was no time to spare; this was an emergency!

Matthew presents the King in control and says in effect, "The Doctor will see you now," as he reported, "He *saw* his wife's mother lying sick with a fever" (Matthew 8:14). The Lord sees His patient through His eyes of compassion and care. Help is on the way.

We would do well to consider each of these accounts in the way we pray for others we should make a request on behalf of someone in need by calling on the Lord to do something with an *"at once"* kind of urgency but also take the time to reassure the patient that the Lord is aware of their need.

Then in the treatment of her sickness, the Gospel writers present differing views. Luke says, "So He stood over her and rebuked the fever, and it left her." Maybe that's the way Dr. Luke would like to treat his patients and bring health and healing to them. As a physician Luke showed great faithfulness in his ministry to the apostle Paul who writes of him, "Only Luke is with me." I also wonder if it was at Dr. Luke's suggestion that the apostle wrote to Timothy to "take a little wine for his stomach's sake" and frequent infirmities.

In contrast, Mark describes the gentle bedside manner of the Great Physician as "He came and took her by the hand and lifted her up and immediately the fever left her" (Mark 1:31). Mark presents the Lord Jesus as the Servant and in this case describes His helpful way of lifting her up. May we, too, follow this example in our service to others.

It was Matthew who mentioned His touch saying, *"So He touched her hand, and the fever left her"* (Matthew 8:15). The medical community has made such strides in their high tech, computerized, voice-activated equipment that sometimes we are **out of touch**. We need both, don't we? High tech and His touch administered through loving physicians who care. Thank God for caring nurses and physicians who see the importance of the Lord's care and compassion and show it so tenderly to their patients. They are an example to other medical workers and a comfort to all of us in times of sickness. The King, as Matthew presents the Lord Jesus, has every help at His disposal and can bring all power together **in a touch**.

James tells us what to do whenever anyone in our local fellowship is sick (James 5:14-15). *"Is anyone among you sick? Let him call for the elders of the church, and let them pray over him, anointing him with oil in the name of the Lord. And the prayer of faith will save the sick, and the Lord will raise him up."* The anointing oil wasn't something mystical or magical but, more than likely, was medicinal. Just as on many mission fields today, the elders of the church are the ones to go to for medical help. We go to the doctor when we are sick, and so we should. We also ask for prayer, and, ultimately, James says, *"The prayer of faith will save the sick, and the Lord will raise him up."* That's what He did for Peter's mother-in-law.

Yes, the Gospel writers give us a full picture from their differing points of view. Notice the one thing they all state is how she responded to His touch. She arose and served them. How did she serve? I have no doubt that she served them the wonderful meal that she had prepared. She did what she did best. She fed them!

Every miracle has a message. Even for us today. As we read in the Word of God about the Lord meeting someone's need through His touch, we learn how He meets our need, too.

Just like Simon's mother-in-law, we want to serve the Lord. We must realize that we have no strength in ourselves. We need His touch. Anything we do for Him must be done by His power. He told His disciples, *"Without Me you can do nothing."* He didn't say, "Without Me you can do some things," but He said, *"Without Me you can do no-thing"* (John 15:5). Oh, listen, we need His touch through His Word in our lives to enable us to serve Him.

How does He touch us today? Do we wait to feel a tingle in our spine before we serve? No. We read that His strength is made perfect in our weakness, and we respond by faith (2 Corinthians 12:9). We act on that same power that raised up Simon's mother-in-law to serve, and then we rise to the occasion that is before us.

The apostle Paul had learned the lesson. Speaking of his ministry, he wrote to young Timothy, *"I thank Christ Jesus our Lord who has enabled me."* Yes, apart from Him we can do nothing, but with Him we can do all things! (Philippians 4:13).

The question we have to ask is, "Am I serving fervently or **feverishly**?" Before you become faint with that fever, labouring in His service, pause and ask Him for His touch. It is through His touch that He supplies strength to serve. Proverbs 24:10 says, *"If you faint in the day of adversity, Your strength is small."*

**Reach Out and Touch Someone!**

# Cleansing the Leper

## The Scriptures

"Then Jesus, moved with compassion, stretched out His hand and touched him, and said to him, 'I am willing; be cleansed.'"
—Mark 1:41

All three synoptic Gospel writers record the miracle of the cleansing of the leper. By reading all three we piece together the details of the event. As you read the Scriptures, notice that Matthew, Mark, and Luke touch the same points in their accounts.

*"And behold, a leper came and worshiped Him, saying, 'Lord, if You are willing, You can make me clean.'*

*"Then Jesus put out His hand and touched him, saying, 'I am willing; be cleansed.' Immediately his leprosy was cleansed. And Jesus said to him, 'See that you tell no one; but go your way, show yourself to the priest, and offer the gift that Moses commanded, as a testimony to them.'"* —Matthew 8:2-4

*"Now a leper came to Him, imploring Him, kneeling down to Him and saying to Him, 'If You are willing, You can make me clean.'*

*"Then Jesus, moved with compassion, stretched out His hand and touched him, and said to him, 'I am willing; be cleansed.'*

25

*"As soon as He had spoken, immediately the leprosy left him, and he was cleansed.*

*"And He strictly warned him and sent him away at once, and said to him, 'See that you say notihng to anyone; but go your way, show yourself to the priest, and offer your cleansing those things which Moses commanded, as a testimony to them.'*

*"However, he went out and began to proclaim it freely, and to spread the matter, so that Jesus could no longer openly enter the city, but was outside in deserted places; and they came to Him from every direction."* —Mark 1:40-45

*"And it happened when He was in a certain city, that behold, a man who was full of leprosy saw Jesus; and he fell on his face and implored Him, saying, 'Lord, if You are willing, You can make me clean.'*

*"Then He put out His hand and touched him, saying, 'I am willing; be cleansed.' Immediately the leprosy left him.*

*"And He charged him to tell no one, 'But go and show yourself to the priest, and make an offering for your cleansing, as a testimony to them, just as Moses commanded.'*

*"However, the report went around concerning Him all the more; and great multitudes came together to hear, and to be healed by Him of their infirmities.*

*"So He Himself often withdrew into the wilderness and prayed."*

—Luke 5:12-16

# The Story

"Unclean! Unclean!" He gagged on those words. It reminded him of his first visit to the priest and the way he used such caution as he looked at his arm. "You won't be going home," he said, "for seven days." The priest wouldn't even look at him. He just said, "You're unclean." He couldn't believe what he was hearing. Maybe the priest was wrong. Time would tell.

The week away from his wife and children seemed an eternity. He passed each day in isolation, waiting, hoping that the sore would just disappear. It didn't. It just stayed the same.

He heard the priest coming his way and raised his arm to him to show that there was no change. "Look, no change. It must be okay," he said, trying to express the relief he felt, but he could tell the priest didn't share his joy. "Another seven days," he said with almost no expression and again he declared, "Unclean."

His sight was blurred from staring at the sore. The third day another sore appeared. It was spreading. When the priest returned at the end of the week, he didn't have to say a thing. The man knew. It was leprosy.

He looked past the priest to his wife and children standing in the distance. The look in her face as she turned to go home broke his heart a thousand times over. He stumbled and fell on the stony ground. The pain was only dull, but he saw his knees and hands bleeding. Even worse was the numbness in his heart. Too sad to even swallow, his mind was racing in a loop echoing the words he had heard, until finally he himself said it, "Unclean! Unclean!"

He thought to himself, "Living outside the city isn't life at all. Separated from everyone and everything. That's what death is, isn't it? Separation. Yes, it's death. Slow and tormenting."

He could see a crowd gathered and wondered what was going on. Was it a riot? No, couldn't be. They were running toward something, not away. They were running toward a person, but to whom?

There was a note. He lived for her letters from home more than the food, left for him at night, that she sent with the children. So, this was what was happening in town. A Healer going through the villages. He read her words, "Sweetheart, I think He can help you." He spoke aloud to himself, "But, why would He? I'm an outcast. An untouchable. No, I don't think He would help me. Even if He could, I don't think He would. Not me."

Two days later he heard another crowd. They were there again. Yes, they were gathering around the Healer. There He was. He wondered, "Should he?" He convinced himself to come a little closer but was careful to keep his distance. Right there; just one step more. He saw the Healer looking his way.

"Oh Lord, please, please," he called. He thought to fall on his knees to reassure the Healer that he would not venture towards Him. "Please, Lord, please! You're my only hope. I won't come any closer. I'm, I'm unclean," he warned. "I know that you can't touch me. You'd be defiled. But, Lord, please if You are willing, You can make me clean."

He kept trying to speak, but the words just wouldn't come. All he could do was stay where he was, waiting, kneeling with his face to the ground. What did he have to lose? Then he felt it. It was a hand, gentle and warm, resting on his shoulder. Someone was touching him, a sensation he had not felt for such a long time, not since he was separated by the priest. He heard His voice saying something. He realized that He was speaking to him. He was saying, "I am willing; be cleansed."

He lifted his face from the ground and saw the skin on his hands was like new. His knees were not red, and his feet could feel the sand between his toes. Toes! He had toes again! He could stand. The healer was speaking to him, but he could hardly listen for the joy of being whole. All he could think about was going home.

Oh, he heard what He said, "Don't tell anyone, but go and show yourself to the priest, offer a sacrifice, as Moses commanded, as a testimony to them." However, the last person he wanted to see was that priest. He started home, and on the way he could not contain himself. He had to tell it. The priest would hear soon enough. He would offer a sacrifice later, but for now all he could think about was that he was cured and going home!

He cut through the market where he used to sell his goods and saw all his friends. They were amazed. Their faces grew bright as they seemed to reflect his own joy to be back within the city again. All he could say as he passed by them was, "I'm back. I'm well and I'm on my way home!

It felt so good to be home again, just to hold his wife in his arms and to wrestle with the children like they were all a bunch of kids. He was enjoying all the things he had been too busy to do before. The order of the day was to play and live each moment to the fullest, and he loved it!

He thought to himself a few days later, "I should go to the priest, but the Healer hasn't come into town since that day. There are just too many people. They say He comes but stays outside the city, and the people go and meet Him there. I'm sure it works out much better that way. The town can be too crowded. Funny, they say that He is usually seen in the very place He touched me and made me clean. It is like we've traded places. He was in and I was out, but now I'm in and He's out!"

The Healer's words haunted him, "See that you say nothing to anyone..." He pushed the thought out of his mind as he spoke with his wife saying, "I'll never forget His touch. He wasn't afraid. He was willing, and I am clean! I guess that's all that matters. Surely, He'll understand that I didn't do what He told me."

# The Study

II. CLEANSING THE LEPER (Mark 1:40-45; Matt. 8:2-4; Luke 5:12-16)

A. The Request (Mark 1:40)

☙ William MacDonald says that the account of the leper gives us an instructive example of the prayer that God answers. (Believers Bible Commentary p.139)

1. *A leper came to Him* — We should take our requests to the Lord Himself

2. *Imploring* — Our prayers should be earnest out of genuine need

3. *Kneeling down to Him* — We should be humble and honour the Lord

4. *Saying to Him* — We should be direct

5. *If You are willing* — We should ask according to His will

6. *You can* — We should have faith that God is able

7. *Make me clean* – We should acknowledge our own needs

☙ When we pray like this, we know the Lord will hear and answer according to His will (1 Jn. 5:14-15).

B. The Response (Mark 1:41)

1. His compassion — *Moved with compassion*

2. His response — *He stretched out His hand*

3. His touch — *He touched him* (which according to Leviticus 18 would make Him unclean, not to mention the fear of a contagious disease)

4. His will — *I am willing*

5. His Word — *Be cleansed*

C. The Results (Mark 1:42-45)

1. Immediate (Mark 1:44) — This word, immediately, appears 36 times in the Gospel of Mark
   a. The leprosy left
   b. He was cleansed
   c. He was warned — *Tell no one!*
      1) Why?
      2) Obviously, so as not to hinder the Lord's ministry of preaching!
   d. He was instructed – *Go to the priest*
      1) As a test — to the leper
      2) As a testimony — to the priests

2. Eventual (Mark 1:45)
   a. He told — He did not follow the Word of God
   b. He hindered so that the Lord could not move freely to preach
   c. The Lord traded places with this leper

# The Sermon

In the Bible, leprosy is a picture of sin. It rendered the person unfeeling, no longer sensitive to touch. That was the danger of this dread disease, the maiming of the extremities of the body by things like fire and heavy or sharp objects. A person could cut himself with a knife and not even realize it. Leprosy separated him from his family and friends. He lived in isolation with other lepers, outside the city, and was required to warn anyone approaching him that he was, "Unclean, Unclean!"

The first person in the Bible to see leprosy was Moses (Exodus 4:6-7). God told him to put his hand into his bosom, and when he pulled it out, it was leprous. It is a metaphor for what sin is and where it comes from. Sin comes from within. Then his hand being leprous shows that what comes from the heart defiles a man (Mark 7:20). Since we are sinners in our heart, we commit sin with our hands. In other words, what we are determines what we do. We sin because we are sinners.

The Lord cured Moses' leprosy by telling him to return his hand back into his bosom, and when he pulled his hand back out again, it was whole. I'm sure that he was relieved! It is the same with us. Just as the Lord deals first with us in our hearts by cleansing us within, we then demonstrate His cleansing power by our works and new life.

Miriam, Moses' sister, also learned about leprosy when she and Aaron spoke ill of her brother (Num. 12:10). I wonder how many lepers there would be if God acted in this way again. We also see that God kept the Israelites waiting until Miriam was restored. None of us lives to himself or dies to himself (Rom. 14:7). Sin in the camp affects us all.

Naaman the Syrian (2 Kings 5:1-16) came to Israel to be cured of his leprosy, and the king of Israel thought the king of Syria was picking a fight. When the prophet, Elisha, heard about it, he sent for Naaman and healed him without cost, although Naaman offered to leave lavish gifts in appreciation of his healing. Gehazi, Elisha's servant, thought his master was letting the Syrian off too easily. He must have had an eye for nice clothes and lots of silver, so he overtook Naaman and, through deception, asked for a couple of changes of clothes and a talent of silver as payment. He received it, too, but ended up with more than he bargained; he was covered with Naaman's leprosy (2 Kings 5:27)!

The story of the four lepers in the siege of Samaria (2 Kgs. 7:3-9) is my favorite. During the siege they determined that they were going to die of leprosy anyway, so why not go to the Syrian army and surrender. *"If they kill us, we shall only die,"* they reasoned. When they arrived at the camp, they found the Syrian army had fled leaving all their supplies. After feasting from tent to tent, progressive dinner style, these four lepers said, *"We are not doing right. This day is a day of good news, and we remain silent."* They were more sensitive about the Gospel than we are! So, they went and proclaimed the good news. I'm glad they did, and I'm glad that the four Gospel (*good news*) writers did not hold their peace either. Are you silent in this day of *good news*? If we are silent and not sharing the Gospel, we are not doing right!

The New Testament has only two accounts of leprosy being healed. The first is the man whom the Lord touched and healed (Mark 1:40-45). The other account is about ten lepers who were healed (Luke 17:12-19). We also know of Simon, the leper of Bethany, in whose house our Lord dined and was anointed by Mary, but we don't have the account of his healing recorded for us in the Bible (Matt. 26:6).

These two occasions teach us important lessons. The first teaches us about the **will of God** and the second about the **worship of God**. We're especially interested in the first occasion with the man whom the Lord touched and made clean.

All three synoptic Gospel writers record the healing of this man. Luke, being a doctor, tells us the extent of his illness, that he was **full** of leprosy (Luke 5:12). Matthew tells the story, too (Matt. 8:2-4), but Mark's Gospel gives us more detail.

Notice how the leper made his approach to the Lord, coming, imploring, and kneeling down to Him. He makes his request saying, *"If You are willing, You can make me clean."* How much we learn from this man's example! He was convinced that the Lord was able — *"You can."* It wasn't a question of His power but rather of His will. *"If You are willing."*

Mark also records the Lord's willing response in a wonderful way. He was *"moved with compassion, stretched out His hand and touched him, and said to him, 'I am willing; be cleansed'"* (Mark 1:41).

The results were immediate, and he was cleansed.

The results were also instructive. Jesus strictly warned him not to make it known, but he went out and began to proclaim it freely and to spread the matter (Mark 1:45).

Think about God's will in this miracle. Before you say that you want God's will for your life, you need to know what God's will is. You can be sure that His will is the best plan for your life. He created you and He knows what is best. What does the Bible say about God's will?

We know, based on the Scripture, that His will is for your salvation.

- It is God's will that you are born into His family - Speaking of those who receive Him as their Saviour, John writes, *"Who were born, not of blood, nor of the will of the flesh, nor of the will of man, but of God"* (John 1:13). God wants you in His family.

- It is God's will that everyone comes to Him - The apostle Paul writes, *"For this is good and acceptable in the sight of God our Saviour, who desires* [wills] *all men to be saved and to come to the knowledge of the truth"* (1 Tim. 2:3-4).

- It is not God's will that any perish - *"The Lord is not slack concerning His promise, as some count slackness, but is long-suffering toward us, not willing that any should perish but that all should come to repentance"* (2 Peter 3:9).

The same as this man wanted God's will for his life, at least with respect to being cleansed from leprosy; you should want God's will for your life, the salvation of your soul.

Another part of the will of God is our sanctification - *"For this is the will of God, your sanctification: that you should abstain from sexual immorality"* (1 Thes. 4:3). Our lives should be set apart, different, just for Him! The Lord Jesus prayed to the Father, *"Sanctify them by Your truth. Your Word is truth"* (John 17:17).

How would you say this man responded to the sanctification part of the will of God?

The leper wanted His will for cleansing, but he didn't follow His Word. The Lord said, *"See that you say nothing to anyone; but go your way, show yourself to the priest, and offer for your cleansing those things which Moses commanded, as a testimony to them,"* but he did not obey Him.

How are we sanctified, set apart for God? We are sanctified by His Word. Did you know that the Lord Jesus prayed this for you? In His high priestly prayer, the Son of God asked the heavenly Father to *"sanctify them by Your truth."* Then He went on to declare, *"Your Word is truth"* (John 17:17). In other words, He prayed that our lives as believers would be different than before and different than the world by being obedient to the Word of God.

In short, God wants you in **His will** and in **His Word**!

This man wanted His will for cleansing, but then he wasn't obedient to His Word. I wonder how many can relate to this kind of thinking. It's really playing a game with God, but He's not fooled. The fool is the one who would want His will but not His Word. James warns us to *"be doers of the Word, and not hearers only, deceiving yourselves"* (Jas. 1:22).

There are other facets of His will, like doing good that you may put to silence the ignorance of foolish men who might accuse you of doing wrong (1 Pet. 2:15). Then God's Word goes a step further and adds suffering for doing good is also part of His will (1 Pet. 3:17). On top of all that you might experience in knowing and doing the will of God, He also tells us to be thankful, *"for this is the will of God in Christ Jesus for you"* (1 Thes. 5:18). My attitude should be one of thankfulness — in everything!

Now, wait just a minute, you say. You mean God's will is more about how I live than where I live? That is right. God's will guarantees us the best plan for our lives:

- Eternally—Salvation
- Outwardly—Sanctification and how to suffer—for doing good and not evil
- Inwardly—Thanksgiving

But what about where I should go to school and live and work and who I should marry, and how many children should we have in our family and all the rest? This is the beauty of the will of God. If you follow the will of God that is written in the Bible, as we have noted, He will make known to us His will in every decision of life. Proverbs 3:5-6 says, *"Trust in the Lord with all your heart, And lean not on your own understanding; In all your ways acknowledge Him, And He shall direct your paths."*

Back to our friend who wanted the will of God without the Word of God. The Lord's command not to make it known was, of course, so that His ministry would not be hindered. The Lord's instruction to go and show himself to the priest had a two-fold purpose. It was a test and a testimony, a test of the man's obedience for it was a Levitical requirement and a testimony to the priest. This probably would have been the first time a priest would have seen someone healed of leprosy. It would have been a testimony to him that the Messiah had come. (Matthew 8:4)

Do you want God's will for your life? You'll find it in God's Word. Oh, you say, "There is so much I don't understand." There is still a lot that I do not understand, but I have learned that if I will do God's will that I will know His Word. It works both ways. Jesus said, *"If anyone wants to do His will, he shall know concerning the doctrine"* (John 7:17). If you will spend time in the Word of God, you'll know His will and have a life that is set apart (sanctified) for the Lord. If you do not spend daily time in the Word of God, you will never have a life that will count for the Lord. What you learn by reading the Bible, you must be willing to live. As you live, you will learn more and more.

A leper was ceremonially unclean, separated from home, and forced to live outside of the town in deserted places. The Lord healed him, and he went around proclaiming the news on his way home… to the city. The end result was that the Lord

Jesus traded places with the leper. The leper had been out of the city, and the Lord had been in. Because the Saviour was willing, the leper was now in the city, and the Lord was out! Now the Lord Jesus could no longer preach in the city where the leper had broadcast the news, but rather He was outside in the deserted places. *"Surely He has born our griefs and carried our sorrows"* (Isa. 53:4).

"Wait a minute!" you say. "Are you suggesting that Jesus took **my** place? That He traded places **with me**?" Yes, that is exactly what He did for the leper and also for us. He took our place — there on Calvary's cross. We should have been crucified, suffered and died, but He suffered and died as, *"the just for the unjust that He might bring us to God"* (1 Pet. 3:18). We deserved death, the death of the Cross, and He deserved glory and honour. He was righteous and holy and has traded His righteousness for our sin; He died that we might live. He was nailed to the Cross that we might go free!

Nance and I have had the privilege to meet some very dear people who had leprosy. During our missionary service in the Ituri Rain Forest of Zaire, Africa, we visited a mission station called Lolwa. After speaking that Sunday morning, we were invited to visit the lepers who lived outside the community in a camp on the outskirts of the mission station.

As we made our approach to the camp, we heard the excitement of the people calling to the others, "They're coming! Hurry! They're coming!" As we entered through the gate, each person greeted us one by one, bowing and thanking us again and again for coming to visit them. The first lady to extend her hand to me had no fingers. She reached out a nub of a hand. I took hold of her wrist ever so gently and greeted her.

I could not help but think about the Lord and His touch. His touch brought healing. Oh, that our touch might at least bring comfort. As I greeted and bowed to them, I saw that some had no toes but rags and blood-stained bandages around their feet using a stick to balance themselves. We were blessed to have met them. They were the most grateful and gracious people we have ever had the pleasure to have met. I look forward to seeing them again in glory with brand new bodies, all because He is willing.

So, we have **touched** on a lot of things here that we can call, "Lessons from a Leper." The main thing, of course, is God's will. God has a will and way to give you the very best life. He is able and He is willing. Are you?

### He Touched Me!
# Raising the Dead

## The Scriptures

"Then He came and touched the open coffin, and those who carried him stood still. And He said, 'Young man, I say to you, arise.'"                                    —Luke 7:14

Only Luke records the miracle of raising the widow's son from the dead. In the beginning of his book, Luke gives an explanation worth noting. He writes, *"Inasmuch as many have taken in hand to set in order a narrative of those things which have been fulfilled among us, just as those who from the beginning were eyewitnesses and ministers of the Word delivered them to us, it seemed good to me also, having had perfect understanding of all things from the very first, to write to you an orderly account, most excellent Theophilus, that you may know the certainty of those things in which you were instructed"* (Luke 1:1-4).

Luke, being a doctor, had made careful investigation of the events in the life of the Lord Jesus. He made sure that he had perfect understanding, an orderly account, and the certainty of those things. He did indeed. Then he put the events in an orderly fashion as they fit categorically. He did this so that we may have confidence in what we find in his Gospel. Knowing this makes me look forward to what we are about to read. Do you?

*"Now it happened, the day after, that He went into a city called Nain; and many of His disciples went with Him, and a large crowd.*

*"And when He came near the gate of the city, behold, a dead man was being carried out, the only son of his mother; and she was a widow. And a large crowd from the city was with her.*

*"When the Lord saw her, He had compassion on her and said to her, 'Do not weep.'*

*"Then He came and touched the open coffin, and those who carried him stood still. And He said, 'Young man, I say to you, arise.'*

*"So he who was dead sat up and began to speak. And He presented him to his mother.*

*"Then fear came upon all, and they glorified God, saying, 'A great prophet has risen up among us"; and, "God has visited His people.'*

*"And this report about Him went throughout all Judea and all the surrounding region."* —Luke 7:11-17

# The Story

Alone, the widow was all alone. She never thought it would be this way. She tried to sort out her thoughts, but with the endless stream of neighbours, her thoughts were put on hold. All she could manage now was the next thing —washing the body of her son. Her hands trembled as she manipulated the arms and legs of his cold, lifeless body. His skin was smooth, no marks of aging like hers, yet colourless as death.

The blanket she had woven for his bar mitzvah would have to serve as his casket. That was the best she could do. Her friends would understand. They knew how hard life had been for her, a widow, to raise a son. "We got by," she thought to herself. There was always some way they had made it. But what now? There was no one to help. Her hope was gone. She'd watched him struggle to draw his last breath. This was no time to think about the future. Today, I have only today. My son, my only son, is gone, and I am alone, all alone.

The crowd was exuberant. They had left Capernaum that morning with new life in their step for the things they had seen the day before. The long walk seemed like nothing as they listened to His parables and teachings along the way. As they saw the city of Nain in the distance, their enthusiasm revived. Someone struck up a song, and they quickened their pace, walking in time and clapping out each beat. They knew that many in the city had heard Him before. If not, everyone surely knew about the Prophet from Nazareth. They hoped their show of support for His ministry would draw many more to follow from this little city.

"They are here, the pall bearers," spoke the solemn voice from outside her door. She was startled back to reality. She would take one last look and try to imagine his bright smile. How she would miss him! As they covered his face, once full of life, she could still picture those curious eyes looking up to her as if she had all the answers. He always had so many questions, non-stop. She usually did have the answers or, at least, could make him think so. Until now, she realized. Now she had more questions than answers. As they lifted his body onto the carrier, she cried in a whisper, "I was all he had. He was all I had."

The crowd seemed to carry her along against her will. Each step grew heavy with sorrow, and she felt that she had slowed down the procession to a standstill. They were not moving, she realized. Fear swept over her; were they already at the tomb? She looked through her tears to see the city gate looming before her as a threshold unto death. She saw the figure of a man with His hand touching her son. He was saying something. He was speaking to her. "Do not cry," He said. With a voice that seemed to soothe her pain, He called again, "Woman, do not weep."

The wailing and mourning of the comforters combined with joyful singing in the distance faded from her hearing. Then a hush fell like a breeze that cut through the day and just one voice was all she heard; that same voice that had told her not to weep was now saying to her son, "Young man, I say to you, Arise!"

She sat right down in the street, and pushing back her hair from her face, strained to see as her son's body arched to life and he sat up. Was He alive? Could it be? No one spoke except the young lad. "Mother!" he cried. "What's going on? What are we doing here?"

Just then the Man lifted the boy from the carrier. The boy's arms wrapped around His neck, and he buried his face against His shoulder as if embarrassed by the crowd. The Man brought him to his mother who was still sitting, unable to move, and with the semblance of presenting a newborn baby, He handed him to her waiting embrace. She received him as a priceless gift, and the lad started in with his questions, talking non-stop. There was no doubt that her son was alive again! She could hear over his constant chatter, the singing starting up again with the whole city of Nain joining in. The funeral dirge had shifted from a minor to a major key.

# The Study

III. RAISING THE DEAD (Luke 7:11-17)

A. Circumstances (Luke 7:11-12)

1. Journey to Nain—a long day's journey from Capernaum (Luke 7:11)

2. Death—a circumstance we must all someday enter, unless our Lord comes first (Luke 7:12)

B. Compassion—*"Do not weep!"* (Luke 7:13)

1. The Lord saw her—What a comfort! (Luke 7:13a)

2. He had compassion on her – What a consolation! (Luke 7:13b)

3. He said to her, *"Do not weep!"* (Luke 7:13c)—What a thing to say to someone grieving! Are we not supposed *to "rejoice with those who rejoice and weep with those who weep"*? (Rom. 12:15) Only the Lord of life could speak this way.

4. He came and touched the bier upon which the young man lay. (Luke 7:14a)

C. Command—*"Young man, I say to you, arise!"* (Luke 7:14b)

D. Comparisons (Luke 7:12)

1. Two Only Sons (Luke 7:12c)

   a. The Lord—The only begotten Son of God

   b. The lad—The only son of his mother, and she was a widow (Luke 7:12c)

2. Two Large Crowds (Luke 7:11-12)

   a. Jesus' group—*"**many** of His disciples ... and a **large** crowd"* (Luke 7:11)

   b. The funeral procession—*"And a **large** crowd was with her"* (Luke 7:12)

43

   3. Two Directions
      a. One going in
      b. One going out
   4. Two Experiences
      a. Jesus' group—Life—joy, gladness, wonder
      b. Funeral procession—Death—sorrow, sadness, grief, mourning
E. Considerations
   1. One gate at the city of Nain
   2. Which gives way? – *"Death is swallowed up by life"* (1 Cor.15:54; 2 Cor.5:4)
   3. Which group are you in?
F. Conclusion—The Lord had said, *"Young man, I say to you, arise!"* (Luke 7:15)
   1. He sat up and began to speak. (Luke 7:15a)
   2. The Lord gave (presented = *did'omi*, same as in John 3:16, *"that He **gave** His only begotten Son"*) him to his mother as a wonderful gift—just like salvation

# The Sermon

What a picture Luke gives through his narrative! Notice the comparisons in Luke's account.

There were two **only sons**, the Lord Jesus who is the **only begotten** of the Father and the lad, the **only son** of his mother who was a widow.

There were two large crowds. One was a funeral procession and the other, a large crowd with many disciples walking from Capernaum with the Lord.

They were going in two directions. One was coming into the town and the other, going out of the town.

There were two experiences. One crowd experienced joy and gladness over the miracles performed by the Lord in Capernaum. The other crowd experienced sorrow and sadness, grief and mourning, in the funeral procession at Nain.

It was life and death, converging at one gate through which all must pass, for death is the threshold to your eternal destination. It is the reality that we will all face if our Lord be not come, for *"it is appointed for men to die once, but after this the judgment"* (Heb. 9:27).

The question is where will you spend eternity? It depends on whose group you are in. If you have come into a living relationship with the only begotten Son of God, Jesus Christ, then you have already passed from death to life (1 Jn. 3:14). You will enter through the gate of death into His presence forever. However, if you do not have the Son, then you do not have life. You will pass through to eternal death (1 John 5:12).

There are two groups of people in the world. One is living; the other is dying. In which group are you? In Adam, our human family head, all die. In Christ all shall be made alive (1 Cor. 15:22). There are only two destinations in eternity. One is Heaven; the other is Hell. Where will you spend eternity?

Yes, life and death met that day at the gate of the city of Nain. Who would give way to whom? Would death or would life give way to the other? The apostle tells us the answer. *"Death is swallowed up in victory"* (1 Cor. 15:54) *"that mortality may be swallowed up by life"* (2 Cor. 5:4).

How do we see life prevailing over death at the gate of the city of Nain? Just look at the way the Lord Jesus moved into the situation. You might say He stopped the funeral procession **dead in its tracks**. What looked to be a finishing touch turned out to mess up a picture perfect funeral. Then He told the boy's mother not to weep! I thought you were supposed to *"weep with those who weep."* Not so for the Lord of life! He touched him, brought him back to life, and gave him to his mother as a priceless gift of life.

This was not the only time the Lord of life interrupted a funeral with a resurrection. After this, He raised a little girl from the dead. She was only twelve years old, the only daughter of Jairus, the ruler of the Capernaum synagogue. Jesus arrived at Jairus' house where everyone was crying and mourning. When the Lord told them not to weep, that the little girl was not dead but only sleeping, they ceased their crying and laughed Him to scorn. The laugh was on them when they found out their mourning services were no longer needed. Jesus sent them all out of the room, took the little girl by the hand, and lifted her out of death and back into life! Then He commanded that she be given something to eat; maybe one of the mourners could go for food (Luke 8:41-42, 49-56).

*"Don't weep,"* and *"He put the mourners all outside."* It is obvious that the Lord did not like weeping. Not so fast, the Lord wept. It was at the funeral of a good friend, Lazarus. The shortest verse in our English Bible says, *"Jesus wept"* (John 11:29). I say it is the shortest verse in our *English* Bible, but it is not the shortest verse in the Greek New Testament. That verse is found in 1 Thessalonians 5:16, *"Rejoice always."* What a contrast! Two short verses give us a brief synopsis; our Savior wept that we may rejoice evermore!

At Lazarus' funeral, the Lord Jesus arrived four days after his death. His sisters had already buried Lazarus. It was too late, or so they thought. *"Show me where you have laid him,"* He said, and standing outside the tomb He commanded, *"Take away the stone."* Martha, Lazarus' sister, tried to stop Him saying, *"Lord, by this time there is a stench."* Martha may have still been talking when the One who is the **Resurrection and the Life** was interrupting. *"Lazarus,"* He shouted, *"Come forth!"* Lazarus came forth wrapped in grave clothes from head to toe. "Loose him and let him go," was the command given by the Lord, and Lazarus walked away from his own grave.

These three occasions when the Lord Jesus raised someone from the dead teach us what our response should be as those whom *"He made alive, who were dead in trespasses and sins"* (Eph. 2:1). The young man whom the Lord touched began to speak, and we, too, have a story to tell. The young girl was raised to life again, and He commanded that something be given her to eat, so we must feed on the Word of God. Then Lazarus, bound by grave clothes, was loosed, and he began to walk. We are to walk, the apostle Paul exhorts, in the newness of life (Rom. 6:4).

The Lord Jesus touched more than just the young man that day. He touched the lives of the people of that region and beyond. Even **you** have heard about it. It is more than a touching story. Have you responded to His touch? Don't wait until you get to the gate!

# He Touched Me!
# Healing the Deaf-mute & Restoring the Servant's Ear

## The Scriptures

"And He took him aside from the multitude, and put His fingers in his ears, and He spat and touched his tongue."
—Mark 7:31-37

"And He touched his ear and healed him."  —Luke 22:51

The Scriptures are from two writers and on two separate occasions. There are two points of contact, the tongue and the ear, but both make up the single process of communication. In the first case, the ears are closed up, and in the other, an ear is cut off. In both there is healing in a touch from the hand of the Maker of us all.

*"Again, departing from the region of Tyre and Sidon, He came through the midst of the region of Decapolis to the Sea of Galilee.*

*"Then they brought to Him one who was deaf and had an impediment in his speech, and they begged Him to put His hand on him.*

*"And He took him aside from the multitude, and put His fingers in his ears, and He spat and touched his tongue.*

*"Then, looking up to heaven, He sighed, and said to him, 'Ephphatha,' that is, 'Be opened.'*

*"Immediately his ears were opened, and the impediment of his tongue was loosed, and he spoke plainly.*

49

*"Then He commanded them that they should tell no one; but the more He commanded them, the more widely they proclaimed it.*

*"And they were astonished beyond measure, saying, 'He has done all things well. He makes both the deaf to hear and the mute to speak.'"*

—Mark 7:31-37

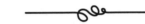

*"And while He was still speaking, behold, a multitude; and he who was called Judas, one of the twelve, went before them and drew near to Jesus to kiss Him.*

*"But Jesus said to him, 'Judas, are you betraying the Son of Man with a kiss?'*

*"When those around Him saw what was going to happen, they said to Him, 'Lord, shall we strike with the sword?'*

*"And one of them struck the servant of the high priest and cut off his right ear.*

*"But Jesus answered and said, 'Permit even this.' And He touched his ear and healed him."*

—Luke 22:47-51

# The Story

"I want to thank you for listening to me so patiently as I have shared with you about how my life was changed forever." His words reverberated off the stone walls in the ancient city. "I look forward to greeting each of you personally," he said as he closed his speech.

He really had held their attention with his eloquence and clarity of speech. The crowd dispersed, and as the young man started to descend the cobblestone street, a couple made their way to him to invite him to their home. They wanted to hear more about him and how he had overcome such great obstacles in his life.

"You see," he proceeded, "I was born here in the region of Decapolis. I was deaf and mute. I lived the first years of my life in the frustration of a silent world. All I could make were noises mostly out of anger and rage. Sometimes I would become so frustrated that I would open my mouth and scream. I knew I got their attention because they looked my way, but they would just stare.

"I studied their expressions and the movement of their mouths. I could mimic them to a tee, but they still could not understand me. I could feel the vibration of my voice, but there is more to communicating than just making sounds.

"My family handled it all right. My older brother, two years my senior, was the best when it came to understanding me. He was my interpreter. My parents usually knew what I needed, but sometimes we would reach an impasse, and even my brother could not translate for me. They would start laughing and so would I, and then my laughter would turn to tears, just because I could not make myself understood.

"My teenage years were the most difficult. The biggest challenge was when people would not even acknowledge me. They treated me like I was ignorant and backward. They were not willing to take the time to get to know me, and when they conversed about me, it was like I was transparent as if they talked right through me. They didn't care what I had to say. I had to accept my limitations and a limited number of friends.

"When I grew into young adulthood, I was on my own. Although I appeared isolated and ignorant, I pretty much knew what was going on. I just could not get in on it. I had resigned myself to this life but often wondered, 'Why?'

"Then it all changed. Last year He came into the town where I grew up. No, I didn't hear about Him, but I saw what was going on with my own two eyes. He was Jewish, but I could see that He was different. There were not many Jews in the area of Decapolis, but He was here, and you could tell that He wanted to be. He exemplified a love for all the people who approached Him. They were mostly people who were challenged in some way like me. There were people who were crippled, sick, and even the strange ones that everyone else avoided. They all came to Him, and the ones that could not come in their own strength were carried on stretchers. Amazingly, He healed them all!

"As I watched one day, I saw Him put His hand on a poor old woman's back who had been bent over for years. She straightened right up, and the crowd, I could tell, was cheering. Then a man I had known in my own community, whose left leg was deformed and had walked with a stick all his life, dragged himself up to Him. He put His hand on the man's thigh, and I watched as the deformed leg gained strength right in front of my eyes!

"I could see everyone's enthusiasm. Even I could not help but open my mouth as wide as ever and just make my usual obtrusive sounds. Then all attention turned toward me. I was almost embarrassed, but there was too much at stake. They were pointing my way, and His eyes were clearly fixed my direction. Would He know my problem? My brother was not there to translate for me. There was no one who would speak up for me. There was just the crowd, and all were waving Him toward me.

"Suddenly I felt someone's hands on my shoulder. A small group of people came up behind me and escorted me to Him. I could tell they were pleading my case, as it were. Then He took me aside. I wondered what was going on. Why didn't He just strike His hand over me and make me whole?

"We walked a few more steps moving away from the crowd. I started to grow concerned that He was going to send me on my way without helping me, but then, He stopped, turned me facing Him. I could see everything He was doing.

"He reached up and put His fingers in my ears, ever so gently. It spoke volumes to me. I realized that He knew that I could not hear a sound. He was aware. I had never felt so relieved or secure, to have someone communicate in a way that I could understand.

"Then holding my face with His hands and keeping my gaze stayed on Him, He spat. I was watching Him so intently that when He spat, I stuck my tongue out as if to do what He did. At that moment, He reached over and touched my tongue. I knew what was about to happen. The thrill was beyond my wildest imagination.

"Then He looked up as if to pray. When He turned His gaze back to me, He had a serious expression. I could see His mouth move as He sighed. I had seen many people sigh before. I knew how it looked and felt. Was He disappointed that His prayer was not answered? What did it mean?

"But then, He spoke, 'Ephphatha! Be opened!' At once I could hear a hollow sound of wind rushing through my ears. It was sound for the first time. My ears were opened, and I made my usual noise, but it wasn't just the vibration of my voice. I could actually hear myself speak from within and without. 'I can hear! I can hear!' I shouted.

"The people came running to us. They were so excited. He tried to calm them down. He was telling them that they should not tell anyone, but the more He said it, the more people gathered. There was no stopping the momentum of that crowd. They were chanting, 'He has done all things well, the deaf to hear and the dumb to tell!'"

The inquiring couple looked at each other in amazement. They marveled as to how the Lord Jesus had touched this man's life. They, too, agreed that the crowd was right, "He has done all things well!"

# The Study

IV. HEARING RESTORED (Mark 7:31-37; Luke 22:9-51)

    A. Healing of the Deaf-Mute (Mark 7:31-37)

        1. Prior Events

            a. After He had been rejected by His family (Mark 6:1-6)

            b. From Tyre and Sidon where He met the Syrophoenician woman—A Gentile— (Mark 7:24-30)

        2. The Place – The midst of Decapolis = Ten cities— among the Gentiles

        3. The Problem (Mark 7:32a-b)—He lacked one of his five senses: Touch, Taste, Smell, Sight, and Hearing

            a. The man was deaf—He could not hear (Mark 7:32a)

                1) He was Isolated—Alone in a silent world

                2) He was Ignorant—Never knowing what was going on around him

            b. The man was mute—Probably a result of the deafness (Mark 7:32b)

        4. The Power (Mark 7:32c-34)

            a. Contrary to their thinking (Mark 7:32c)

                1) The people's way— *"They begged Him to put His hand on him"*

                2) The Lord's way—Communicating by dramatic presentation to this man what He was about to do for him

                    a) He took him aside—He could not tell him, but He could take him

                    b) He put His fingers in his ears—He could

        not hear His Word, but He could feel
fingers in his ears

   c)  He spat—as if to say, you are going to be
able to talk

   d)  He touched his tongue—The man could
not speak, but he felt His touch on
his tongue

  b.  Compassionate (Mark 7:34)

     1)  He sighed = Lit. He groaned!

     2)  He said—"*Ephphatha!*" = Aramaic,
Be opened!

✣ The Gospel of Mark uses three Aramaic expressions
and gives the translation each time. The other two are
worth consideration. (Mark 5:41; and 15:34)

  c.  Complete (Mark 7:35)

     1.  He could hear

     2.  He could speak plainly, too!

B.  Healing of the Servant (Luke 22:47-51)

  1.  The Swordsman (Luke 22:47, 49-50)

    a.  From sleeping (Luke 22:46)

    b.  Asking permission, but not waiting for an
answer (Luke 22:49)

    c.  To swinging one of the two swords the disciples
had (Luke 22:50; 22:38)

  2.  The Servant of the high priest (Luke 22:50)

    a.  His name was Malchus

    b.  His right ear was cut off

  3.  The Sovereign (Luke 22:51a)—"*Permit even this*"
shows the Lord in control!

  4.  The Saviour (Luke 22:51b)—One who sympathizes,
heals, and restores with a touch

# The Sermon
## *The Healing of the Deaf-Mute*

The Gospel of Mark is the only one of the synoptic Gospels that records the account of the healing of the deaf-mute. Some of the details of this event are very instructive.

The setting was in Decapolis which was an area in Syria on the eastern side of the Jordan River made up of ten cities whose population was primarily Gentiles. The healing of this man who was deaf comes after the Lord's visit to Tyre and Sidon where He granted the request of the Syrophoenician woman to heal her daughter. The importance of this connection is that the Lord was reaching out to the Gentiles.

That the Lord is reaching out to the Gentiles does not surprise the Bible student who remembers the promise made to Abraham that all the families of the earth would be blessed through his Seed, Christ. It should not seem strange that the Lord would reach out to the Gentiles based on Isaiah's prophecy that the Messiah would be *"a Light to the Gentiles"* and that He would extend His *"salvation to the ends of the earth"* (Isa. 42:6; 49:6).

How fitting that the miracle would involve hearing. Even the apostle Paul reflected on his ministry saying, *"The Lord stood with me and strengthened me, so that the message might be preached fully through me, and that **all the Gentiles might hear"** (2 Tim. 4:17), and hear they did. The word, *Ephphatha,* is Aramaic for, "be opened," and their ears and hearts were opened by His touch.

Mark keeps the Aramaic rendering of the word, *Ephphatha.* The use of Aramaic is unique to Mark's Gospel. This is one of the three times he renders an expression of the Lord Jesus in Aramaic. The other two are at the raising of Jairus' daughter when He said, *"Talitha, cumi"* (= My little lambkin, arise!), and on the cross when He cried, *"Eloi, Eloi, lama sabachthani"* (= My God, My God, why have You forsaken Me?). In all three occasions Mark is careful to give us the phrase in its Aramaic rendering and then to include the translation for us. These are more than just expressions that Mark chose to leave in their original language form, but the three make up quite a lesson for us to hear (*Ephphatha*) and be made alive (*Talitha, cumi*) through the One who was forsaken for us (*Eloi, Eloi, lama sabachthani*).

The Lord worked contrary to the thinking of the Gentiles, too. They begged Him to put His hand on the man who was a deaf-mute. He took him aside. This would be no sideshow but rather a show of compassion. Our Lord still works contrary to our thinking. The Lord sighs here and only one other place, in Mark 8:12, when they were seeking a sign because He, Himself, was not enough. We, too, sigh when people won't simply take Him at His Word but want something more than to respond in faith. When the Lord Jesus sighs here in Decapolis, it was a prayer that this man's ears might be opened. Again, we, too, should pray for others that they might open their ears to hear.

The Lord could not tell the deaf man what He was going to do, but He could take him aside. The man could not hear, but he could feel His fingers in his ears. He could not speak, but he saw the Lord spit as if to assure him that soon he, too, would be able to "spit it out." Next, He touched his tongue and communicated with this man what no one else could or would.

It is likely that the man's speech impediment was due to his deafness. He could not hear and therefore could not speak. That might be our problem, too. If we want to have something worth saying, we need to listen to His voice through His Word. A friend became weary of hearing his co-worker rattle on and on about nothing and finally exclaimed, "Listen, Joe, if you're going to keeping talking, you're going to have to say something!"

Consider the importance of our senses. Which of the five senses, touch, taste, smell, sight, or sound, do you value most? Many would value the sense of sight above sound, but in the realm of faith that is not, let's say, very **sensible**.

The world says, "Seeing is believing," while the Lord says, "*Believe and you will see*" (John 1:50; 11:40). Remember how Thomas declared, "*Unless I see in His hands the print of the nails... I will not believe.*" When he did see the Lord and was told to look at His hands and to even reach forth his finger and then his hand and to believe, the Lord's words to him include a blessing for us today. He said to Thomas, *"Because you have seen Me, you have believed. Blessed are those who have not seen and yet have believed"* (John 20:29).

The other senses such as taste may not be worth considering since some people have no taste at all. How about smell? You are thinking there are times that it may be beneficial to give up smell, but seriously, even smell offers us much to enjoy in life.

Touch and feelings often are confused in matters of spiritual things. It is good to remember that touch and feelings are more tied to that which is soulish and oriented to our emotions while that which is spiritual is communicated through the Word of God by the Spirit of God to our spirits.

Our current expressions in our English language often lead us astray, do they not? We say, "I *just feel* this way about the Lord," when that may not be in accord with the Scriptures at all. A quick look at Genesis 27:21-27 will reveal the misuse of every sense except for the most important one. It is in the story of Jacob and Isaac and the procuring of the blessing that we find the key. The deceiver, Jacob, deceived his father Isaac through his **sight** that was dim, the **taste** that he thought was venison, the **touch** that passed goat's hair for Esau's arm (I would hate to meet him on a dark night), and **smell**, meaning that Esau must have smelled like a goat! The only thing that Isaac was right about was the **sound** of the voice being that of Jacob, but he went by his other senses and rejected what he heard.

So, which will you follow? Go by your sense of sound for the Bible says, *"Faith comes by hearing and hearing by the Word of God"* (Rom. 10:17). Now that, by the way, makes good *sense*.

The Lord Jesus offered a parable to illustrate the importance of hearing. In the parable of the Sower, He compared four different kinds of hearers to four types of soil. One was hard soil, hard of hearing, as indifferent to the message. The next fell upon rock. The soil was shallow, and the seed sprung up quickly, as emotional hearers. The third fell among thorns and was being choked out, as the worldly hearers. The last was good soil and yielded a crop a hundredfold. The seed sown was the Word of God, and it bore fruit only in one kind of soil, the good soil –those who heard (Luke 8:4-8)!

He finished that parable with an exhortation, *"He who has ears to hear, let him hear!"*

Then He followed the exhortation with an explanation of the parable to His disciples who just could not understand it. To help them, and us, too, He spoke another parable about a lamp. He pointed to those who light a lamp and put it under a bushel or a bed rather than on a lampstand. The idea is that some people are too busy to listen in the case of the bushel while others are too lazy to listen as in the case of the bed. The lamp should go on a lampstand for all to see, but before you draw the natural conclusion for clear sight, the Lord gives a similar exhortation, *"Therefore take heed how you hear"* (Luke 8:18).

Two parables, both emphasize being careful to interpret correctly what one is hearing.

Then, in God's precise timing, the Lord's mother and brothers arrive. Due to the crowd, they send in a messenger to tell Him that they are standing outside, desiring to see Him. The Lord, as the Master Teacher, turned the interruption into an illustration and said, *"My mother and My brothers are these who hear the Word of God and do it"* (Luke 8:19-21).

The problem with mankind is not that we cannot hear the Word of God. It is that we do not hear and, in some cases, will not hear God speaking to us. We, as it were, hold our hands over our ears refusing to listen when only through the hearing of the Word of God can we have life, for *"faith comes by hearing, and hearing by the Word of God* (Romans 10:17).

## The Healing of the Servant

The other occasion of the Lord touching someone's ear took place in the Garden of Gethsemane when a mob came to arrest Jesus. All four Gospel writers include this account of the cutting off of the ear of the servant of the high priest. Taking all four accounts will give you an earful.

Luke describes the chaotic scene of the disciples waking

from their sleep and rushing headlong into the fray, calling out, "Lord, shall we strike with the sword?" Unfortunately, they did not wait for an answer. We know that there was more than one sword on site from Luke 22:38 where the disciples have two swords, not to mention the swords and clubs of the mob that came to arrest Him.

Neither Matthew nor Mark tell us that it was Peter who was the swordsman, but they do let us know that it all took place suddenly, and that the one who was struck was the servant of the high priest. John gives more detail in that he names Simon Peter and the servant whom he struck, Malchus. John also mentions that it was the right ear that was severed (John 18:10).

Peter, a better fisherman than swordsman, no doubt went for Malchus' head, who probably ducked. Instead of murder, Peter cut off his ear. The Lord quelled the storm with three words, "Permit even this."

Matthew tells us that He rebuked Peter saying, *"Put your sword in its place,"* and warned him that those who take up the sword would die by the sword. This reminds us that the weapons of our warfare are not fleshly, rusty swords but the sword of the Spirit which is the Word of God. The Lord Jesus explained that at that very moment He could call on the Father who would provide twelve legions of angels. Our Lord exercised great restraint submitting Himself into the hands of sinful men all the while committing Himself to the Father who judges righteously. (1 Peter 2:23)

Peter won the argument, made his point, but lost the battle. He was fighting the Lord's battle with the weapons of the flesh. We do the same thing sometimes and cut people's ears off with our sharp words. Then we have to ask the Lord to put their ear back on so we can try again to share the good news. That is the point, is it not? We must spread the message to the world around us. *"He that has an ear, let him hear"* is the call for the attention of people's hearts.

It was Peter, on the Day of Pentecost, who skillfully wielded the sword of the Spirit that day and they were *"cut to the heart"* (Acts 2:37). The response of the people that day was wonderful.

They said to Peter and the rest of the apostles, "Men and brethren, what shall we do?" Their ears were opened by the Word of God and to the message of the Gospel.

Only Luke, the doctor, tells us about the **outpatient surgery** of reattaching the ear instantly by His touch. We read that the Lord *"touched his ear and healed him"* (Luke 22:51). It would give the old advertisement, "And now, from the Maker of Miracle Ear" a real setting for their jingle.

Our Lord is not only the great Physician, but He also performed the first surgery. In the Garden of Eden He caused a deep sleep, better than anesthesia, took a rib from Adam, performed re-constructive surgery from that rib to make Eve, and closed up the incision in Adam's side. That was all done as **Same Day Surgery**. Compared to that, the ear didn't even require an office visit! It was healed with the touch of His hand.

Opportunities come in unusual places like the hospital visit Nancy and I made to a dear friend, Paul, who had a very serious surgery. After his surgery, we went to the hospital to visit him. Prior to his surgery they removed his hearing aids. He didn't even hear us come into his surgical recovery unit. We touched his arm, and he opened his eyes. Unable to speak, he motioned that he wanted to write a note. I gave him my pen and the back of a receipt. He scribbled the word, D-o-x-o-l-o-g-y.

We read his scribbling and mouthed the word, doxology. He shook his head, "Yes!"

"You mean you want to give God the glory for bringing you through the surgery?" we asked.

He shook his head, first "Yes" and then "No."

"Do you mean that you want us to sing the Doxology?"

"Yes," he shook his head again to say, "Yes!"

We looked at each other, and I started the song. Nance joined in, *"Praise God from Whom all blessings flow;"*

At that Paul took his hand and cupped his ear as if to say, "Louder." So we brought it up a notch, *"Praise Him all creatures here below;"*

Again, with his hand cupping his ear, we took it up another level, *"Praise Him above ye heavenly hosts;"*

Finally, with both hands behind his ears and a smile on his face, we sang as loudly as we could, *"Praise Father, Son, and Holy Ghost! A - men."*

I'm not sure if Paul heard us sing the Doxology that day, but everyone else on the Third Floor, D-wing did!

We have a message to tell a noisy, busy world. It seems that everybody is talking, but nobody is listening. They need His touch to open their ears to hear the Word of God. He is reaching out to touch someone today – through you and me. How? Take some time to be quiet in God's presence and listen to His voice. It is written in black and white and hopefully **read** every day. As we read the Word of God, we hear what God has to say. Then, like the man who was deaf and mute, we will hear His Word and speak His message using *"great plainness of speech"* (2 Cor. 3:12).

I trust you noticed the connection of the two men who had their ear problem corrected. One has to do with hearing His voice while the other has to do with spreading the message. Both are needed for our communication to the world around us, and both require a touch from the Lord for the message to penetrate hearts.

# He Touched Me!

# Calming Fears

## The Scriptures

"But Jesus came and touched them and said, 'Arise, and do not be afraid.'"
—Matthew 17:7

Three men with the Lord on the holy mount and three Gospel writers tell the story.

*"Now after six days Jesus took Peter, James, and John his brother, led them up on a high mountain by themselves; and He was transfigured before them. His face shone like the sun, and His clothes became as white as the light.*

*"And behold, Moses and Elijah appeared to them, talking with Him.*

*"Then Peter answered and said to Jesus, 'Lord, it is good for us to be here; if You wish, let us make here three tabernacles: one for You, one for Moses, and one for Elijah.'*

*"While he was still speaking, behold, a bright cloud overshadowed them; and suddenly a voice came out of the cloud, saying, 'This is My beloved Son, in whom I am well pleased. Hear Him!'*

*"And when the disciples heard it, they fell on their faces and were greatly afraid.*

*"But Jesus came and touched them and said, 'Arise, and do not be afraid.'*

*"When they had lifted up their eyes, they saw no one but Jesus only.*

*"Now as they came down from the mountain, Jesus commanded them, saying, 'Tell the vision to no one until the Son of Man is risen from the dead.'"*
—Matthew 17:1-9

"And He said to them, 'Assuredly, I say to you that there are some standing here who will not taste death till they see the kingdom of God present with power.'

"Now after six days Jesus took Peter, James, and John, and led them up on a high mountain apart by themselves; and He was transfigured before them.

"His clothes became shining, exceedingly white, like snow, such as no launderer on earth can whiten them.

"And Elijah appeared to them with Moses, and they were talking with Jesus.

"Then Peter answered and said to Jesus, 'Rabbi, it is good for us to be here; and let us make three tabernacles: one for You, one for Moses, and one for Elijah' — because he did not know what to say, for they were greatly afraid.

"And a cloud came and overshadowed them; and a voice came out of the cloud, saying, 'This is My beloved Son. Hear Him!'

"Suddenly, when they had looked around, they saw no one anymore, but only Jesus with themselves."                    —Mark 9:1-8

"Now it came to pass, about eight days after these sayings, that He took Peter, John, and James and went up on the mountain to pray.

"As He prayed, the appearance of His face was altered, and His robe became white and glistening.

"And behold, two men talked with Him, who were Moses and Elijah, who appeared in glory and spoke of His decease which He was about to accomplish at Jerusalem. But Peter and those with him were heavy with sleep; and when they were fully awake, they saw His glory and the two men who stood with Him.

"Then it happened, as they were parting from Him, that Peter said to Jesus, 'Master, it is good for us to be here; and let us make three tabernacles: one for You, one for Moses, and one for Elijah' — not knowing what he said.

*While he was saying this, a cloud came and overshadowed them; and they were fearful as they entered the cloud.*

*"And a voice came out of the cloud, saying, 'This is My beloved Son. Hear Him!'*

*"When the voice had ceased, Jesus was found alone. But they kept quiet, and told no one in those days any of the things they had seen."*

—Luke 9:28-36

# The Story

"I remember the experience like it was yesterday," John said, as he continued to reminisce to a handful of young men who had come to visit. "It started with a trip up north to Caesarea Philippi.

"Philip was enthusiastic as he was getting ready for our trip. 'Vacation time and we're ready!' he said.

"'Vacation?' Thomas quipped.

"'Okay, so it's not a real vacation. It will still be a break,' Philip responded, so as not to be dissuaded. 'Think of it this way,' Philip went on, 'It'll be great just to get away, refresh, and regroup. You know what they say —*a change of scenery is a rest*!'

"Arriving, Thomas called back to Philip, 'Talk about a change of scenery... I mean, look at all those idols! No wonder pantheists claim that god is in everything; they're all over the place! Tall, short, and in between, whatever size niche is hewn in the side of the mountain, there's a Pan to fill it.'

"Nathanael added, 'I don't expect any good to come out of this place.'

"Andrew chimed in, 'At least it's relaxing here with the coolness of the fresh water springs and the sound it makes dancing over the rocks.'

"Thomas didn't even notice. He just went on in his sarcastic way, 'A bubbling brook is not what I need after the *question and answer* session along the road. What was that all about? Who do they say I am and who do you say I am? And when we finally got the right answer, He told us not to tell anyone? And this talk of going to Jerusalem, I'm telling you right now that we'd better stay away from there or we'll all end up dead!'

"'Wake up everyone,' I called. 'We're going on further today.'

"Thomas moaned, 'Guess it was too good to last.'

"Andrew didn't let it slide by. 'I thought you said it was no good anyway?'

"'No, that was Nathanael,' he barked. 'Where are we going?'

"I pointed to the high mountain in the distance. 'Up there?'

"'Whatever for?' he murmured, shaking his head in disbelief.

"About that time, James came in and told me, 'You weren't to call everyone. It's just you, me, and Simon who are going.'

"I was embarrassed, that is until the rousing started from the others. 'Did your mother put in a good word for her two boys? Be sure to walk, one on His right and the other on His left!' The rest of the disciples jeered, too, while Simon made his way out and over to us.

"The path up the mountain was steep with no even grades for a breather. Every turn just revealed another upward climb with further to go. After walking for some time, I suggested to the Master that we rest a little while. 'That's fine', He said, 'This looks like a good, level spot. We'll stop here for now.'

"We sat, and I pulled out some food and passed it around to share while we rested. The Lord began to explain to us some things that were new and sounded complicated. They were things about the kingdom and coming events. Just the week before He had mentioned something along the same lines about seeing the kingdom before we die. It was like He picked up where He left off.

"We tried to follow, but as we listened we couldn't help but look down over the ridge below. It was beautiful. There was a gentle breeze that seemed to brush over us, just enough to make us comfortable as we listened. I guess we became a bit too comfortable.

"Simon was sitting beside me, and he seemed earnest as if hanging on every word. That is until I noticed his sigh of agreement waned, fell silent, and turned into soothing sounds, and eventually he started to snore. I jabbed him in the side, and he sputtered a bit, leaned over on his hip and was soon fast asleep. James was sleeping, too. I was the only one still awake, but in the quietness of the setting, I could feel myself drifting. I remember hearing the Lord begin to pray. I was trying to follow what He was praying, but I just couldn't hold my eyes open.

"I awoke startled, and Simon was standing, kind of staggering. I figured that he must have been awakened, too. There was a light, bright and white like the sun. It was coming from the Lord's face and even His clothing. I couldn't gather my thoughts quickly enough to discern what was happening. Then I noticed in the glory of His light that there were two men beside Him, talking together with Him. They looked strangely familiar, although I knew that I'd never seen them before. They had to be Moses and Elijah. You could tell. They looked bold and glorious like the stories we had heard as boys.

"As they were talking to the Lord, I strained to hear what they were saying. Simon interrupted with words that seemed slurred and confused. 'Lord, it is good for us to be here.'

"'What?' I wondered. 'I'm not even sure where *here* is!'

"Simon went on, as if to fill in the empty space brought on by his interruption. 'Let us build three booths. One can be for You, one for Moses, and one for Elijah.' Well, at least Simon identified the two ancient visitors the same as I thought them to be.

"The words were just out of Simon's mouth when a cloud enveloped us with a thickness we could feel. From all around us we heard a voice speaking in sure tones. God had come down on that mountain and spoke saying, 'This is My beloved Son. Hear Him!'

"I looked at Simon who had fallen prostrate on his face. I, too, lay low and glanced at James who had never even gotten up. We all were shaking, too terrified to move. Then I felt the pressure of a hand on the back of my shoulder. It was His hand touching me to reassure me that all was well, and we were safe. I heard the kindness of His voice as if He had Himself experienced a great struggle. 'Arise,' He said, 'and do not be afraid.' I heard Him saying the same to Simon and to James.

"As I turned to look, expecting to see more light and the two visitors, they were gone. I saw only the Lord. We were speechless, even Simon! We gathered our things and began to descend the slope. About halfway down, the Lord broke our silence by telling us in no uncertain terms that we should not tell this vision to anyone. 'Not until the Son of Man is risen from the dead,' He added.

"His words concerning the Son of Man being raised from the dead only added wonder to the surreal experience. Having initiated the conversation, we started right in with some of our questions about the teachings of the Scribes, the end times, and the coming of Elijah. Yes, we saw the light all right, and things were beginning to dawn, but we understand so much more now that He is risen, just as He said."

# The Study

V. CALMING FEARS (Matt. 17:7-9)—Disciples on the Mount of Transfiguration

   A. The Setting (Matt. 17:1)

      1. The Persons—Peter, James, and John

      2. The Place—On a high mountain (Mt. Hermon is the highest in the area)

      3. The Purpose—Prayer (Luke 9:28-29)

   B. The Sight (Matt. 17:2-3)

      1. A true view of the King (Matt. 17:2) transfigured = *metamorphosed*

        a. First His face *"shone like the sun"*

        b. Then His clothes *"became as white as the light"*

      2. A preview of the kingdom (Matt. 17:3)

        a. The companions – Moses and Elijah

          1) The kingdom represented

            a) Moses representing the Law

            b) Elijah representing the Prophets

            b) Peter, James, and John representing the NT saints

          2) The subjects of the kingdom represented

            a) Moses—Those who will be raised from the dead

            b) Elijah—Those who will be raptured

            c) Peter, James, and John representing the remnant when He comes!

          3) The visitors themselves

            a) Still living

            b) They were recognized; no introduction

was necessary

   c) They could speak to each other

   d) They knew about coming events

   e) They were not afraid of the glory of Christ

   f) They communed with Christ

  b. The Conversation (Matt. 17:3) — *"Talking with Him"* (Luke 9:31)

   1) His death and departure — *"spoke of His decease"*

   2) His work — *"which He was about to accomplish at Jerusalem"*

C. The Statements (Matt. 17:3-7)

  1. The Disciples — Peter acts as their spokesman

   a. First sleeping (Luke 9:32)

   b. Then speaking (Matt. 17:4)

  2. God (Matt. 17:5-6)

   a. A Divine Interruption — *"while he (Peter) was still speaking"*

   b. A Divine Introduction — *"This is My beloved Son"*

   c. A Divine Imperative – *"Hear Him!"*

   d. A Divine Impact – *"They fell on their faces and were afraid"*

  3. The Lord Jesus (Matt.17:7-9)

   a. Calming Touch — *"But Jesus came and touched them"*

   b. Comforting Word — *"Arise, and do not be afraid"*

   c. Conclusive Look — *"They saw no one but Jesus only"*

   d. Commanding Restraint — *"Tell the vision to no*

*one until the Son of Man is risen from the dead"*

✌ Peter did just that and learned from it an important lesson (2 Pet. 1:16-18)

# The Sermon

The Lord Jesus is moving closer to Calvary as He travels each step of the way with His disciples. There are many things to teach them to prepare for their ministry ahead. In a careful reading of the context in all three synoptic Gospel writers, you will notice the setting is exactly the same. There are three events that stand out in each of the accounts. This is rare and very instructive.

The three events take place at Caesarea Philippi and on a high mountain. Firstly, the Lord Jesus establishes the confirmation of His identity. *"Who do men say that I, the Son of Man, am?"* (Matt. 16:13-16; Mark 8:27-30; Luke 9:18-22). Their response was varied, but when asked specifically, *"Who do you say that I am?"* Peter made the confident confession, *"You are the Christ, the Son of the living God."* This, by the way, was declared with a backdrop of a solid stone mountain with numerous niches hewn in the rock, each housing an idol of the false god Pan. What a setting for such a statement of the identity of our Lord, the Christ, the Son of the living God!

Remember the description of the psalmist concerning these dead idols. *"Their idols are silver and gold, The work of men's hands. They have mouths, but they do not speak; Eyes they have, but they do not see; They have ears, but they do not hear; Noses they have, but they do not smell; They have hands, but they do not handle; Feet they have, but they do not walk; Nor do they mutter through their throat. Those who make them are like them; So is everyone who trusts in them"* (Psalms 115:4-8).

Secondly, He tells of His suffering which He would suffer in Jerusalem. He is on His way to the cross. Then He challenges His disciples to count the cost, deny themselves, and take up the cross and follow Him. This exhortation still echoes in our hearts to this day knowing what our Saviour endured for us.

King of my life, I crown Thee now,
Thine shall the glory be;

Lest I forget Thy thorn-crowned brow,
Lead me to Calvary.

May I be willing, Lord, to bear
Daily my cross for Thee;
Even Thy cup of grief to share,
Thou hast borne all for me.

Lest I forget Gethsemane;
Lest I forget Thine agony;
Lest I forget Thy love for me,
Lead me to Calvary.

—Jennie Evelyn Hussie

Thirdly, He showed His kingdom glory in preview form. He had promised just days earlier that there were some that were present who would not taste death until they saw the Son of Man coming in His kingdom (Matt. 16:28). These three, Peter, James, and John, were those who were chosen to see His glory and kingdom previewed.

These three events give us a basis that we should take to heart. First, consider who He is, then what He did, and finally, how He will come. He is the Son of God who gave Himself for us and will come again in glory!

The disciples, Peter, James, and John, like David's three mighty men who were loyal servants to their king, were often present with the Lord Jesus at momentous events in His life and ministry. They were with Him at the raising of Jairus' daughter, they were here at the Transfiguration, they were on the Mount of Olives (with Andrew accompanying), and at Gethsemane He drew them further along with Him to watch and pray. Why them? Were they closer than the others? Surely, He cared the same for all His disciples, but these three must have drawn closer to Him on their own accord. He graciously included them. He still does. This example makes me want to draw closer and stay close to Him; does it you?

We read that He took them up to a high mountain to pray. There is some debate over which mountain it was, whether Mt. Tabor or Mt. Hermon. Mt. Hermon seems to be the mount where He placed His transfiguration. It is the highest in Israel. At an altitude of 9,232 feet above sea level, it is snow-capped most of the year. Its melting snow combined with the mountain springs are a main source of the Jordan River, and, most importantly, it is nearer to Caesarea Philippi. We don't read that they necessarily went to the top of the mountain, just up on a high mountain and apart by themselves. What a view! However, the purpose was not the view, but the preview, a preview of His glory and coming kingdom.

The synoptic writers each describe Him in their own characteristic way. Matthew and Mark mention that His face shone, as if the veil of human flesh was pulled back for this short preview, and they saw Him as He is (Matt. 17:2; Luke 9:29). Mark writes that His clothes became shining, exceedingly white, like snow, such as no launderer on earth can whiten them (Mark 9:3). Leave it to Mark, from his servant's perspective to present Him in the cleanest clothes ever. It was the meek and lowly Jesus —high and lifted up in His Glory. He was *transfigured* before them. He was *transformed*, metamorphosed, which is the Greek word equivalent used by the synoptic Gospel writers.

Although John did not include the event in His Gospel account, he did write, *"We beheld His glory, glory as of the only begotten of the Father, full of grace and truth"* (John 1:14). How does all this affect me? Paul helps us in the application as he later writes, in 2 Corinthians 4:6, *"For it is the God who commanded light to shine out of darkness who has shone in our hearts to give the light of the knowledge of the glory of God in the face of Jesus Christ."*

This *preview* of the kingdom was complete in two ways. Depicting the kingdom, Moses and Elijah appeared with Christ. Moses, representing the Law, and Elijah, representing the Prophets, and Christ the King, were joined by the disciples, sleeping as they were, but representing the New Testament saints. You also can see in Moses those represented who have died and were raised, while Elijah pictures those who will not die yet go into glory at the Rapture. The disciples, therefore, picture the faithful remnant that will be living when the Lord Jesus Christ comes in glory and power.

I marvel at the power of God who *"is not the God of the dead, but the God of the living"* (Mark 12:27). Moses and Elijah need no introduction. They are very much alive, conversing with each other and with the Lord Himself concerning His decease which He was about to accomplish at Jerusalem. His decease which He would accomplish is none other than the finished work of Christ at Calvary. This was the Father's plan which the Son fulfilled. The counsels of heaven were known by the heavenly visitors but still in mystery form to the disciples at that time.

Three voices were heard on the Mount of Transfiguration. Although there was a conversation between the Lord and the two visitors, the first voice we hear is that of Peter. We are not surprised. In fact, Mark tells us plainly that Peter did not know what to say, and Luke concludes that Peter did not know what he said (Mark 9:6; Luke 9:33). Do you ever feel that way? Sometimes we are not sure what we should say, and we open our mouths and remove all doubt. That was the case this time for Simon Peter. He said, *"Lord, it is good for us to be here."* That was a great start, but it was pretty much downhill from there. James 1:19 tells us that we should *"be quick to hear and slow to speak."*

Peter not only has something to say, he always seems to have a plan. He offers, *"Lord, if You wish, let us make here three tabernacles: one for You, one for Moses, and one for Elijah."* While it was nice of him to start with the Lord, he did err when he seemed to place them all on the same level. Christ should have the preeminence in all things. As the writer of Hebrews properly compares the Lord Jesus to angels, prophets, and priests and declares Him to be much better, yes, even greater than all (Heb.1:4; 4:14).

The other problem with Peter's plan was that they were not there to stay. We cannot stay on the mountain top either. We often enjoy mountain top experiences of our time with the Lord personally or at conferences and camps with fellow believers. Often, when the experience is over, we come down to find challenge or even conflict. The mountain top times are necessary, but we do not want to be ignorant of Satan's devices. Learn from this experience as the disciples come down to conflict and must again depend on the Lord to bring clarity out of chaos (Luke 9:37-42).

While Peter was still speaking, the next voice sounded. It was a Divine interruption from God who spoke out of the cloud which had suddenly overshadowed them, saying, *"This is My beloved Son, in whom I am well pleased. Hear Him!"* We read in Hebrews 1:1 that God spoke at various times and in various ways in time past. One of those ways He spoke in Moses' days at the tabernacle was out of the cloud, and here again He speaks the same way. Now, as His voice from the cloud introduced, in these last days, He has spoken to us by His Son (Heb. 1:1-2).

God's message was clear. He confirmed that the Lord Jesus is His beloved Son and that they should listen to Him. This voice was from heaven just as it was at our Lord's baptism when the Father spoke in this same fashion. The Father loves the Son and gladly announces that Jesus Christ is His **beloved** Son. Wonder of all wonders, the **love** that He has for His Son is the same that He has for us! The Lord Jesus said, *"As the Father has loved Me, even so have I loved you"* (John 15:9). And again He assures us saying, *"The Father Himself loves you"* (John 16:27).

The difference in the content of His words at our Lord's baptism and on the Mount of Transfiguration is the addition, *"Hear Him!"* The point is, "Peter, hold your peace! Listen to My Beloved Son!" To which we all should concur as we sit in His presence. Not as Israel said, *"Let not God speak to us!"* But, rather as Samuel responded, *"Speak, Lord, Your servant is listening."* Let us give credit to Peter who did get it right when he said, *"Lord, to whom shall we go? You have the words of eternal life"* (John 6:68). Peter would have done well had he listened to his own confession.

As the voice came from the bright cloud, it must have reverberated all around them being enveloped by the cloud. So terrifying was the experience that the disciples fell on their faces and were greatly afraid. The last voice they heard was the familiar one they knew well. The Lord Jesus came and touched them, and when they looked up, they saw Jesus only. He told them not to be afraid. Someone has counted three hundred sixty seven *fear not's, do not fear's,* or *be not afraid's* in the Bible. That is one for everyday of the year, plus two more for leap year. This is one of those times when they needed to hear His *fear not.* His Word assures and His touch reassures them that they have no need to fear. What calm and comfort there is in His touch. John experienced this again in Revelation 1:17 when he saw the Lord Jesus and fell at His feet as dead, and He placed His right hand on him and said, *"Do not be afraid."*

Just as He warned His disciples at Caesarea Philippi not to make known His identity, He also warned these three to tell the vision to no one until the Son of Man is risen from the dead. They followed this command, and Peter spoke at the appropriate time and in a most powerful way saying, *"For we did not follow cunningly devised fables when we made known to you the power and coming of our Lord Jesus Christ, but were eyewitnesses of His majesty. For He received from God the Father honour and glory when such a voice came to Him from the Excellent Glory: "This is My beloved Son, in whom I am well pleased." And we heard this voice which came from heaven when we were with Him on the holy mountain"* (2 Peter 1:16-18).

What does this mean for us? No, you and I were not on that mountain seeing a preview of His glory, but we do have His prophetic word confirmed as we read Peter's eyewitness account. The Lord of glory did not touch us as He did those disciples on that day, but as we take heed to His Word in our hearts, it brings comfort and calm to our lives just as real as His touch, maybe even more so.

# Let the Little Children Come!

## The Scriptures

"Then they brought little children to Him, that He might touch them." —Mark 10:13

The Scriptures are from two writers, Mark and Luke. They say essentially the same except that Mark includes the blessing of the children. Brief as they both are, they speak volumes on the importance of children and the lessons we learn from them.

*"Then they brought little children to Him, that He might touch them; but the disciples rebuked those who brought them.*

*"But when Jesus saw it, He was greatly displeased and said to them, 'Let the little children come to Me, and do not forbid them; for of such is the kingdom of God. Assuredly, I say to you, whoever does not receive the kingdom of God as a little child will by no means enter it.'*

*"And He took them up in His arms, put His hands on them, and blessed them."* —Mark 10:13-16

*"Then they also brought infants to Him that He might touch them; but when the disciples saw it, they rebuked them. But Jesus called them to Him and said, 'Let the little children come to Me, and do not forbid them; for of such is the kingdom of God. Assuredly, I say to you, whoever does not receive the kingdom of God as a little child will by no means enter it.'"* —Luke 18:15-17

## The Story

"Are the children with you?" Tom called to his wife. She heard the tension in his voice, coming from the challenge of getting the family ready to go.

"No," she paused, "I thought they were with you, dear." Her words floated down from the loft with softness intended to turn away wrath. She'd learned this from her mother-in-law during their first year of marriage when they lived at home while building their house. It worked every time.

"Okay, Joanna," he replied with a calmer tone. "Are you nearly ready?"

"Almost," she said, smiling to herself.

Just then Tom heard the children outside. There was no doubt about it being his children. He could identify each voice and each laugh; Sally with her chuckle mixed with daring tones, Thomas in his own inimitable way, Suzie, although just three years old, the little mother commanding the others to play nicely while Ben mocked her, taunting her to try to catch him.

Heading out the door, with each step a long stride, Tom made his way to the corner of their home, leaned around the stones, and demanded that they come immediately into the house to get ready to go. "We should be leaving now!"

"But, Father, do we have to go?" Suzie whined.

"Well sure, sweetheart. We're going together as a family to see the Teacher from Galilee on His way to Jerusalem," her father explained.

"Why?" she cried.

Tom knew the problem. He knew that the children feared the rabbis at the synagogue. Many times the Pharisees and Sadducees had evidenced that they didn't want the children around. "Children should be seen and not heard!" was often what the children heard from the leaders. They didn't have to say it; the children could see it, the scowl on their faces whenever the children came near.

Tom reassured Susie and all the children. "I hear that this Teacher is different," he said. "Why, up in Galilee, rather than send the multitudes away, He fed them, all of them, with just two fish and five loaves!"

"How many people were there?" Sally asked.

"Five thousand and that was counting only the men!" Tom asserted.

"Impossible!" Ben exclaimed.

"That's what I heard, and the source was quite reliable," Tom stated as a final word in the conversation. "Okay, up and into the house with all of you, and, get ready now; we're going!"

As he turned to go back into the house, he thought to himself, "Lord, how blessed I am! I have a wife, a family, and our home, right here with all our relatives living within shouting distance. Within shouting distance is right", he confessed, "and, Lord, I know I need to do a little less shouting these days. Please help me in this. Amen."

"Well, is anyone coming with me to see the Teacher?" Tom called. With that, Joanna walked into the room, followed by the girls, while Thomas and Ben came running down the steps from the loft bounding right into the middle of the room. "Okay, let's go!" he said.

Joanna cleared her throat and whispered, "Tom, aren't you forgetting something?" Embarrassed, he nodded his head to acknowledge, "Oh, yes, thanks, sweetheart. Who wants to pray for our trip today?"

Ben said, "I prayed yesterday."

The girls added their response, "Thomas. Let Thomas pray this time."

Thomas folded his hands and bowed his head. They all formed a little huddle as he prayed in measured tones, "O Lord, thank You for today. Thank You for our father and mother and for my brother and sisters. Thank you for the beautiful day and for letting us go to see the Teacher who is coming through our village today. Lord, we pray that we might get close enough to touch Him. Amen."

Tom felt badly, but he had to tell the children. He knew they would be so disappointed if they couldn't see Him, so he said, "Thank you, Thomas, for praying, but I want you children to know that it will be very difficult to greet the Teacher. There'll be a lot of people, and we'll be blessed if we are even able to see Him!"

Sally asked, "Well, what's the point of going if we can't meet Him?"

"Yea," Susie, chimed in.

"You're right," their father said, taking the cue from Joanna. "Let's go in faith and hope for the best! Thomas has prayed and we believe; right?"

"Right!" they all said in unison.

As they made their way over the brow of the hill, they could see the crowds of people. They wondered if they were too late. The multitude seemed to flow through every crook and over every slope of the hills like a field of wheat blowing in the breeze. The Pharisees were standing over to the side, together, in deep conversation, arms folded and faces stressed like they were plotting something in secret. They were easy to spot and just as easy, thankfully, to avoid.

"There He is, the Teacher!" shouted Thomas. "Over there, coming up from the grove of trees."

"Yes, that must be Him and his disciples," confirmed Joanna, "and look at the crowd walking along with Him already."

"Can we go meet Him?" Sally asked.

Her father looked her way and shook his head. "Not yet, Sally. It looks like the Pharisees are going to meet with Him first."

"Guess they'll get the first word," Tom mumbled to himself. "It's for sure that He'll get the last word, or so I hear."

Tom and Joanna saw some friends and neighbors from the village. As they greeted one another, the children began to play together while they waited. They had a lot in common with many of the families there. The parents were committed to raising their children in the nurture and admonition of the Lord. They had taught them the Scriptures and were working with them to memorize entire books of the Pentateuch. They considered the opportunity for their children to meet the Teacher as a once in a lifetime event.

Just then, the Teacher turned to walk away from the Pharisees. All could tell it had not been a pleasant conversation. He looked up and saw the families just up the hill from Him and seemed to be glad that they were there. The children noticed Him, too. Then, He smiled a big, inviting smile. That was all the children needed. They stopped their games, and in one seemingly choreographed movement, they began running towards Him.

The disciples panicked! They started to form a line of protection in front of the Teacher as if to fend off an attack. One of them, the big, burly one, shouted at the parents, "Get these children out of here!" The parents stood speechless as if frozen in place. Then, the Teacher stepped through the disciples. He said something to His disciples which must have been a rebuke, judging by their response. They just hung their heads in shame.

The line of defense quickly transformed into a circle of love. The Teacher opened his arms wide to the children as they made their way to Him. He picked up little Suzie in His arms and holding her on His side, He placed His right hand on Thomas' shoulder. The children were thrilled and so were Tom and Joanna that the Lord had answered their prayers, especially Thomas' prayer which he prayed early that morning to be able to be close enough to touch Him.

Then the children sat and listened as He spoke to their little group and His followers. What profound truths He spoke, unlike anything they had ever heard before. He said, "Let the little children come to Me, and do not forbid them; for of such is the kingdom of God."

Gently He picked up one of the little children and went on to teach saying, "Unless you become like one of these little ones, you will by no means enter the kingdom of heaven. And, if you want to become great, you must humble yourself as this little child." As the words left His lips, He turned toward His disciples to be sure that they understood the message. Then He smiled again, blessed the children, and stood as if He was pressed to leave. The families took the signal that their visit was over, and it was time to start for home.

As they walked away, Ben skirted around the disciple who had chased them away at first. Ben still wasn't too sure about him, that is, until the disciple stooped over and held out his hands as if to apologize. Ben, though cautious, could see he was sincere. The big man had learned a lesson, and although Ben was a little boy, he was big enough to forgive and trust him. Instead of taking his hands, Ben jumped up and hugged his neck. Waving good-bye, Ben ran quickly to catch up with his family as they headed home.

"Well," Tom said, "We got close, didn't we?"

"Yes, Father," Sally sighed, "we got close enough to touch Him!"

Thomas slipped over behind his mom and said, "But He touched me first."

About that time Ben came running by and said, "Here's a touch: tag, you're it!" And Thomas chased him all the way home.

# The Study

VI. BLESSING THE CHILDREN (Mark 10:13-16;
Luke 18:15-17)

  A. What it tells us about parents (Mark 10:13)

    1. They brought their little children to Him

      a. They didn't *send* them, they *brought* them

      b. They started bringing them when they
were *little*

    2. They sought His touch for their children—His
blessing on their lives!

  B. What it tells us about the disciples (Mark 10:13b)

    1. They didn't always understand—Sometimes
we don't understand either

    2. They didn't see the profit and benefit of ministry
to children

    3. They are a good example of what *not* to do!

  C. What it tells us about children (Mark 10:13 and 16)

    1. They were not afraid to come to Him

    2. They were glad to be picked up and blessed in
His arms

  D. What it tells us about Christ (Mark 10:13-16)

    1. He was approachable (Mark 10:13)

    2. He was indignant with His disciples and took
the opportunity to teach them an important lesson
(Mark 10:14)

    3. He was emphatic to the point of how a person is
saved—coming with the faith of a child
(Mark 10:15)

    4. He was glad to bless, and he enjoyed the children

      coming to Him (Mark 10:16)

E.  What it tells us about ourselves (Mark 10:13-16)

    1.  We should be the kind of people that children want to be around (Mark 10:13)

    2.  We should be burdened for the children in our family and communities (Mark 10:14)

    3.  How we should be as children (Mark 10:15)

    4.  How we should seek His blessing for them through us (Mark 10:16)

# The Sermon

We learn a lot of lessons from these little ones. The first set of lessons is for parents. Just the fact that the parents **brought** their children to Jesus is important. How were you raised? Did your dad and mom send you or bring you to church meetings? More importantly, how are you raising your children? Children learn by example.

Sayings like, "Children should be seen and not heard," and "Do as I say, and not as I do," are not worth the paper on which I've just typed them! Our children will do as we do. They learn by example more than by instruction. They can spot a phony a mile away. In short, make your spiritual life a family matter. Do not **send** your children to Sunday School; **take** them to the meetings. Most importantly, lead them to Christ!

The responsibility of raising our children in the nurture (training) and admonition (warning) of the Lord (Eph. 6:4) is one of great consequence. The problem is that there are no trial runs to raising children. The first time counts. The Lord said of Abraham, *"For I have known him, in order that he may command his children and his household after him, that they keep the way of the Lord, to do righteousness and justice, that the Lord may bring to Abraham what He has spoken to him"* (Gen. 18:19). Namely, he and Sarah would have a son, Isaac. They had waited for years for this blessing. How old was Abraham when he was finally ready to raise his children? Ninety-nine!

It takes a lifetime, a long lifetime, to learn what we need to know as parents when it comes to raising our children. So, what are we to do? Acknowledge our great need to the Lord for His help. Raise our children prayerfully and carefully in the nurture and admonition **of the Lord**. In other words, seek His counsel and follow His Word. Our little and short-lived experience is not enough to get it right. We must grow our children God's way.

In Mark we read that the children were little, and in Luke we read that they were infants. This reminds me that it is never too early to introduce your children to the Lord. If it is never too early to start, then do not wait until it is too late! In one sense we would say that it is never too late, but for the optimum timing in a child's life, the earlier is the better.

I also see that the parents **sought** the Lord's touch and blessing on their children. This is the key. I have read that Susanna Wesley, who had seventeen children, used to spend an hour in prayer for her children everyday, alone shut up in her kitchen. I do not know what kind of children John and Charles might have been, but with seventeen children I might have opted for an hour of quiet time each day, too.

Seriously, think of how the prophet Samuel's mother, Hannah, said concerning him, *"For this child I prayed"* (1 Sam. 1:27-28). Also young Timothy through the influence of the faith of his grandmother, Lois, and his mother, Eunice, (2 Tim. 1:5) from his childhood knew the Scriptures (2 Tim. 3:15) that were able to make him wise unto salvation. Writing to Timothy, Paul now challenges him as a man of God (2 Tim. 3:16). Do you want your children to become men and women of God? Start early. They are like sponges that soak up knowledge in their younger years. The rest of their lives they will be squeezing out the blessing for us all.

Psalm 127 says, *"Children are a heritage from the Lord, the fruit of the womb is a reward. Like arrows in the hand of a warrior, so are the children of one's youth. Happy is the man who has his quiver full of them."*

Children are like arrows. Nancy and I served as missionaries in the Ituri Rain Forest in Africa. We worked among the Pygmies who are sometimes called, "the **children** of the forest." We had the privilege of bringing the Gospel to them and felt that we, in turn, gained much understanding about life from them. The Pygmies are hunters and gatherers. It was in their preparation for hunting that I learned the following illustration for raising children.

I watched as the Pygmies made their arrows for hunting. First they took a scrap piece of metal from an old steel drum. They **shaped** and **sharpened** the arrowhead, just as we must do in our children's lives as we seek to shape and sharpen them. It is the formation and development of their lives in the early stages. Then they took the shaft for the arrow and **straightened** it so that it would fly straight. We, too, must straighten out our children. It is to our children's benefit to discipline them. Chastening is training, not punishment. We are not to be overbearing to the point of exasperating or discouraging our children (Eph. 6:4), but rather point them in the right direction.

After the Pygmy has crafted the arrowhead and shaft, he would make a slit in the opposite end of the shaft and insert a leaf to **stabilize** the arrow in flight. That is comparable, in our example, to reinforce what we have taught. Lastly, they are ready to **shoot**. Someday, we will have to let them go. If prepared, they will fly straight ahead for the Lord.

We also learn something about the disciples. "Get these kids out of here!" Not quite what you would expect to hear in a Church meeting, is it? The disciples missed the point that day when the parents of precious little ones desired the Saviour to bless their children. They did not know the importance of reaching out to children. Sometimes we miss the point, too. I was recently challenged to alter an expression I had used in the past, "Children are the church of tomorrow." Children are not the church of tomorrow. They are the church of today!

Even in our teaching ministry we sometimes have it backwards. We talk up to adults and down to youth. We tend to challenge the adults intellectually and keep our ministry on the lighter side when addressing youth. When will we catch on that young people are sharp and need the challenge? In fact, some young people are more apt to comprehend quicker higher truths than we who are older. Yet, we can learn from the disciples what *not* to do. Pray that the Lord will help us to encourage the children in our families and in our fellowship. Let us learn some lessons from this study before it's too late.

I heard an evangelist give a report at a prayer meeting that three and a half souls were saved through the Gospel campaign. We thought he meant that three adults and one child were saved. We were wrong. It was three children and one adult. A **young** life saved is a **whole** life saved. The half was an adult whose life was already half spent.

We learn something about children from this event. They were not afraid to come to the Lord Jesus. Children love to be loved. They were responsive to the Lord's love and touch. They knew His strength and protection. It could be sensed and felt by them. Remember His warning to those who would cause one of these little ones to stumble? *"It would be better for him if a mill-stone was hung around his neck, and he was thrown into the sea, than that he should offend one of these little ones"* (Luke 17:2). The Lord takes children seriously and we should, too.

This brings us to what we learn from the children about our Saviour. The fact that the children wanted to come to Him tells us that He was approachable. He enjoyed their company, and they enjoyed His. Something surely is amiss whenever those who profess to know the Lord would be otherwise with children. When the disciples rebuked the parents, the Lord rebuked the disciples. We read that He was greatly displeased! That is a strong emotion of indignation. May we take the Lord's reprimand to heart.

We learned a secret from Brother John Bramhall who used to carry candy in his pocket for the kids at the meeting. I remember many times watching a little lad walk up behind him in stealth and reach a little hand into his pocket for his treat. Mr. Bramhall pretended not to notice, but this young fellow knew where the candy was and that he would not be scolded but received with love, Christ's love.

We put this secret into practice in our visits with the Pygmy children. Needless to say, we were a scary sight to these little people of the forest. Learning some of the language was a help to break the ice with the adults, but the children were still skeptical. One day a package arrived from the U.S. We opened it to find a huge bag of hard candy, individually wrapped in cellophane. The following Saturday morning we made our way through the forest to visit the Pygmy camp with a Bible in hand and candy in our pockets. We offered the first candy to one of the children. In no time we were nearly mobbed by all the children in the camp, each with their hands outstretched. The candy went from our hands to theirs and right into their mouths with wonder. A few of the children didn't know to remove the wrapper first. It lasts longer that way, but it is not nearly as sweet. We need to sing more often the children's songs like,

*Jesus loves the little children, all the children of the world.*
*Red and yellow, black and white; They are precious in His sight,*
*Jesus loves the little children of the world!*

And,

*Jesus loves me this I know, for the Bible tells me so,*
*Little ones to Him belong, they are weak, but He is strong.*
*Yes, Jesus loves me; Yes, Jesus loves me;*
*Yes, Jesus loves me; The Bible tells me so.*

The Lord Jesus used a child to teach us that a child doesn't have to become an adult to be saved, but that an adult must become like a child to enter the kingdom of God. What assurance His words give our hearts for those precious little ones who are asleep in Jesus, *"for of such is the kingdom of God."* No doubt and never forbidding, but bidding them to come to the Saviour, He waits for them with open arms of blessing.

Lastly, we learn lessons from the little ones about ourselves. There were two kinds of people on this occasion. There were those who were hard, harsh, and hateful —the disciples, and there were those who were seeking, joyful, and blessed —the parents and children. Which one would you be? Which one should we be?

I know the Bible says, *"**Suffer** the little children,"* and that the old English word, suffer means to allow, but I am afraid that many indeed **suffer** the little children. Do not suffer them, love them. Jesus did. Children are not a burden; they are a blessing. Whenever your smile becomes a scowl, step back and visit this story again. Listen to the Lord's rebuke. Feel afresh His great displeasure and catch the love and joy anew. See life through the eyes of a child and learn the lessons.

If you prefer a quiet gathering over baby sounds of joy, attend more funerals, but, if you want to be teeming with life in the local church, pray for the children in the families of those in fellowship. Seek to win more children to the Lord through showing His love and kindness.

The other day a little girl who is just old enough to say a few words was sitting with her parents at the Lord's Supper. When we passed the bread down her row, she watched as her mom and dad took a piece and passed it by her. She said with her tiny voice, "Bite?" How could anyone be anything but impressed?

Remember that major events like the Passover and placing the stones in the Jordan River and on Gilgal's shore were for the express purpose of teaching the children. That when the children would say, *"What do you mean by this service?"* The parents were to tell them why these events were to be remembered (Ex. 12:26; Josh. 4:6, 21). We are to teach the precepts of the Lord diligently to our children at home, along the way, and to the following generations (Deut. 6:7). Are you stacking any stones along the way or doing anything that would cause the children in your life to ask you about knowing the Saviour?

Let me take nothing for granted here, knowing how seriously the Lord thinks about the care of these "little ones." You see, it is not stacking stones in the Jordan River or celebrating a Passover like the Children of Israel, but allow me to ask about your spiritual involvement with the Lord and His people. We must realize that even if we teach the truth to our children diligently at home, they are also watching what we do. Are we faithful in witness and worship, reaching out and sharing in a fellowship of believers? If not, why not. Your children will do what you do, not what you say.

Finally, we should let Him enfold us with His everlasting arms and lift us up with His joy. Just let Him love you as He really does. Enjoy His touch and fond embrace as we learn some lessons from these little ones.

# He Touched Me!

## Eyes to See

## The Scriptures

"So Jesus had compassion and touched their eyes. And immediately their eyes received sight, and they followed Him."

—Matthew 20:34

Three Gospel writers, Matthew, Mark and Luke, record the healing of blind Bartimaeus and his friend at Jericho. Remember as we read and study that we are drawing close to the end of the life and ministry of the Lord Jesus. He is passing through Jericho on His way to Jerusalem and knows what is ahead. He is ever walking in the shadow of the Cross. May the Spirit of God open our eyes to behold the wonder of it all.

*"And behold, two blind men sitting by the road, when they heard that Jesus was passing by, cried out, saying, 'Have mercy on us, O Lord, Son of David!'*

*"Then the multitude warned them that they should be quiet; but they cried out all the more, saying, 'Have mercy on us, O Lord, Son of David!'*

*"So Jesus stood still and called them, and said, 'What do you want Me to do for you?'*

*"They said to Him, 'Lord, that our eyes may be opened.'*

*"So Jesus had compassion and touched their eyes. And immediately their eyes received sight, and they followed Him."*

—Matthew 20:30-34

*"Now they came to Jericho. As He went out of Jericho with His disciples and a great multitude, blind Bartimaeus, the son of Timaeus, sat by the road begging.*

*"And when he heard that it was Jesus of Nazareth, he began to cry out and say, 'Jesus, Son of David, have mercy on me!'*

*"Then many warned him to be quiet; but he cried out all the more, 'Son of David, have mercy on me!'*

*"So Jesus stood still and commanded him to be called. Then they called the blind man, saying to him, 'Be of good cheer. Rise, He is calling you.'*

*"And throwing aside his garment, he rose and came to Jesus.*

*"So Jesus answered and said to him, 'What do you want Me to do for you?' The blind man said to Him, 'Rabboni, that I may receive my sight.'*

*"Then Jesus said to him, 'Go your way; your faith has made you well.' And immediately he received his sight and followed Jesus on the road."*

—Mark 10:46-52

*"Then it happened, as He was coming near Jericho, that a certain blind man sat by the road begging. And hearing a multitude passing by, he asked what it meant. So they told him that Jesus of Nazareth was passing by. And he cried out, saying, 'Jesus, Son of David, have mercy on me!'*

*"Then those who went before warned him that he should be quiet; but he cried out all the more, 'Son of David, have mercy on me!'*

*"So Jesus stood still and commanded him to be brought to Him. And when he had come near, He asked him, saying, 'What do you want Me to do for you?'*

*"He said, 'Lord, that I may receive my sight.'*

*"Then Jesus said to him, 'Receive your sight; your faith has made*

*you well.' And immediately he received his sight, and followed Him, glorifying God. And all the people, when they saw it, gave praise to God.*

*"Then Jesus entered and passed through Jericho."*

—Luke 18:35-19:1

## The Story

"It's been over three weeks now since my eyes were opened, and what amazing things they have seen!" said Bartimaeus, once known as "Blind Bartimaeus." He made himself comfortable as he sat by the fire on that cool evening in Galilee.

Zebedee and his wife called their children in to listen and asked him to tell his story from the beginning. "Tell us everything," the wife said. The children all scooted up close sitting on the floor around him, prepared to take it all in.

"Jericho was my home. It was where I lived from birth. Of course, I knew it well," boasted Bartimaeus. "I may have been blind, but I knew the city as well as anyone, even those who could see. Every crook and every cranny, every twist and turn, I sensed them, while others only saw them."

"Yes, I was dependent on alms, but I was not undisciplined. Right on schedule, I awoke at the first cockcrow while it was still dark." He chuckled to himself and noted, "It's always dark if you're blind." The children snickered, too, looking at each other as they tried to imagine what life would be like without sight. Bartimaeus continued, "Oh, yes, every morning I would dress, eat, and make my way down the hill. My partner was always waiting for me at the *souk*, and the two of us walked together to our place, just outside the gate. We sat right there against those same stones every day, facing the same way, toward the hill of the gate to the old city."

The old man talked freely as he sat, "We would position ourselves, side by side, legs crossed with a shawl laid out before us, holding just a few coins from passersby. I learned to keep a few coins handy from the day before and place them on my shawl myself. It would draw more alms than a bare cloth." He grimaced and nodded his head, embarrassed to confess what he had learned as a beggar.

"We were a customary sight at the entrance of the city of Jericho, the oldest and lowest city on earth. "On bad days we used to commiserate with each other saying, 'We're as low as you can go, here in the City of Palms,'" as he pointed to his palms to show they were empty. He laughed aloud as he asked the children, "What, did you think the 'City of Palms' referred to the groves planted there?"

"We heard everything, too," he went on. "We couldn't see, oh, but what we heard! You didn't know that about blind people?" he asked the children. "We heard the gossip, the slander. We heard it all; we sometimes even knew what some people were thinking! I still can read minds," he warned as he leaned over to stare into the children's faces as they sat before him, mesmerized, their eyes glaring in amazement. "Like right now," he whispered, "I can hear those wheels turning in your minds as you strain to remember anything you might have said since I arrived this morning." He smiled to reassure them, and then he grew very serious.

"Those days we heard that Jesus was making His way to Jerusalem, and I figured that should bring Him through the very gates where we sat. It thrilled my heart mostly because I knew it was our opportunity to be healed of our blindness, but it also bothered me to know what was ahead for the Messiah."

"There was going to be trouble there, you know, in Jerusalem. There was no doubt about it. We'd heard the rumours. We'd also heard the debate over who He was. Oh, some didn't know, but we did. We were sure He was the One. He was the promised One for whom we'd waited. We heard what He did for those two blind men near Capernaum, how He touched their eyes and made them see! We knew what they said. 'Son of David,' they called Him. 'Have mercy on us,' they cried, and we planned to do the same."

"That day, that wonderful day, my life was changed forever!" Bartimaeus paused to wipe the tears from his eyes.

Zebedee's wife reached over to him to hand him a cloth to wipe his tears, but he did not even notice. He pushed the moisture back to each side of his face and scooted up on the edge of his seat. The children inched closer, too.

"Just then," he said, "there was the sound of clamour in the distance. We listened for clues as to what was happening."

My partner cried, 'What's going on, Bartimaeus?' but I shushed him and leaned forward to listen more in earnest. We heard the sound of a child's feet slapping on the roadway of stone, then another, and another. Until finally we heard many children running ahead of the louder voices and footsteps of men and women as they grew near. We sat still, our heads turned with our ears perked, on alert, toward the direction of the old city."

"Again, my partner called, 'They're just on the other side of the gate, Bartimaeus, They're almost here.' I knew that we had to wait for just the right time. We must catch the first of the crowd, the outskirts of the excitement, or we would get no response."

"The noise echoed as if inside a box and then exploded as the first contingent cleared the city gate, and with perfect timing and a deep authoritative voice, I said, 'What's all the commotion?' The crowd responded as one, 'Jesus of Nazareth is passing by!'"

"The opportunity we had long awaited was here. I called to my friend, 'Now!' I said, 'Now!' And in unison, we cried, 'Jesus, Son of David, have mercy on us! Lord, Son of David, have mercy on us!' The volume of the crowd grew and so did ours as we sounded forth again, 'Have Mercy on us, O Lord, Son of David!'"

"The people continued to pass by, so we began waving our arms and legs and calling out as loudly as we could so as to be noticed. Some from the crowd told us that we were making ourselves obnoxious with our cries. 'Be quiet!' they demanded, but it was like throwing fuel on our fire. There was a fire burning within our souls for years, and it would not be extinguished by someone whom we did not even know telling us to be quiet! We knew at least that we were making ourselves heard. So we cried out all the more, 'Jesus, Son of David, have mercy on us! O Lord, Son of David...' The noise began to subside, but we continued to cry out."

Bartimaeus held their attention and he knew they were hanging on every word. Their expressions changed to one of concern as they thought that the Messiah passed him by with no response. "Just then," raising his voice to surprise them with joy, "someone grabbed my robe. We began shouting again, 'O Lord...,' but they shook us to silence saying, 'Listen, listen for a minute! He's calling you. Jesus is calling you! Cheer up, get up, He's calling you!'"

"I threw aside my shawl, coins rolled every direction, and was on my feet before my partner who was not far behind." Bartimaeus now stood and acted out the motions in dramatic form. "We made our way through the opening in the crowd. It was as if the Lord's gaze had prepared a passageway for us to follow. Coming before Him, we fell on our knees with our faces and hands looking up as if we could see, but we were just facing toward the voice we heard."

The children, Zebedee, and his wife gazed at Bartimaeus kneeling there before them with his hands stretched upward and face gazing toward the ceiling.

He went on to rehearse the events point by point saying, "As He spoke, the crowd grew quiet, 'What do you want Me to do for you?' He asked. Why, that was the easiest question anyone had ever asked me! I answered for us both, 'Master, that our eyes might be opened.'"

"With that the Lord reached down and touched my eyes. I felt His fingers on each side of face and thumbs placed on my eyes closing them ever so gently. When He pulled His hands away I opened my eyes, and immediately I received my sight. The first thing I saw were the palms of His hands, then His face, then His feet as I arose."

The old man got up from his knees, groaned as he came up on one foot and then the other. He stood transfixed, arms outstretched, silently as if waiting for someone to give him permission to continue. "Go on," the children all said, "What happened then, Mr. Bartimaeus?"

"He spoke, gently and directly. His voice swept over me like a breeze, and His words came in deep unto my soul. He said, 'Go your way, your faith has made you well.' We looked at each other, my partner and I. I knew what he was thinking, and I knew that he knew what I was thinking, too."

Bartimaeus paused and asked the children, "I told you that I could hear what people were thinking, didn't I?" They nodded expectantly, waiting to hear what happened next.

"When He told me to go my way, I asked myself, 'What way was that?' My way, until that moment, was in groping in the dark. From then on I wanted to go His way, not mine, and right there and then I determined to follow Him. In fact, we both walked together, my partner and I, with the others. We followed Him to Bethany where they made Him a supper. Then on to Jerusalem when they received Him waving palms and shouting His praise, but, oh what my eyes have seen! In less than a week the crowd that sang His praise turned into a mob poisoned by the scribes and Pharisees, and I saw them with my own eyes take Him out to be crucified. I knew all along that there would be trouble in Jerusalem, but I never thought it could be so bad, and I didn't think it would happen so soon."

"I stayed around Jerusalem for a while with His disciples and the others. I heard that the Messiah had risen from the dead and that He had appeared to His disciples, to some women, and to two other followers on the Emmaus Road. We waited in Jerusalem until someone reported that the Messiah had sent word for us to go to Galilee and that we would see Him there. So, here I am in Galilee with the hope of one more glimpse of the One who opened my eyes and to look once more on the first face I ever saw."

Zebedee and his family thanked Bartimaeus for sharing with them his wonderful story. They assured him that he was their guest and they would be glad for him to stay as long as he liked. Then Zebedee gathered his family together with Bartimaeus and bowed his head and prayed, "Thank you, oh Lord, that one day we all shall see You face to face."

# The Study

VII. SIGHT FOR THE BLIND (Matt. 20:29-34; 9:27-31; Mark
10:46-52; Luke 18:35-19:1)

  A.  The Place (Matt. 20:29)

     1.  Jericho in our time—the oldest city and lowest
city on earth!—850 feet below sea level. It also has
the largest oasis in the world today.

     2.  Jericho in earlier times

        a.  The place where Moses looked into the
Promise Land from Mt. Pisgah (Deut. 34:1)

        b.  The place from where Joshua sent out two men
to spy saying, "Go, view the land, especially
Jericho" (Josh. 2:1)

        c.  It was also there that God promised that
He would begin to magnify Joshua in the sight
of all Israel (Josh. 3:7)

        d.  Finally, it is the place where Joshua lifted his
eyes and saw the Lord Jesus, pre-incarnate, as
the Captain of the host of the Lord (Josh. 5:3)

     3.  Jericho in Jesus' time

        a.  Matthew 20:29 says they were departing
from Jericho

        b.  Luke 18:35 and 19:1 says they were entering
Jericho

        c.  Mark 10:46 says both—"*Now they came to Jericho.
As He went out of Jericho with His disciples and
a great multitude*"

  B.  The People (Matt. 20:29-30a)

     1.  A great multitude followed the Lord (Matt. 20:29)

    2.  Two blind men (Matt. 20:30a)

C.  Their Position (Matt. 20:30b)

    1.  Sitting by the road (Matt. 20:30b)

    2.  Luke tells us that they were begging (Luke 18:35)

D.  Their Perception (Matt. 20:30c)

    1.  *"Have mercy on us"*

        a.  They knew of Him and His mercy

        b.  They had heard what the crowd said, *"And when he heard that it was Jesus of Nazareth,"* (Mark 10:46; Luke 18:35)

    2.  *"O Lord, Son of David!"* — A Messianic title for the Lord Jesus (Matt. 1:1)

E.  Their Persistence (Matt. 20:31)

    1.  The multitude warned them to *be quiet*

    2.  *"They cried out all the more ... Have mercy on us, O Lord, Son of David!"*

F.  The Prayer (Matt. 20:32)

    1.  Jesus stood still — They had the attention and audience of the Heavenly King

    2.  He called them and said, *"What do you want Me to do for you?"*

    3.  Their Request — *"Lord, that our eyes may be opened."*

G.  The Power (Matt. 20:34)

    1.  He had Compassion

    2.  **Touched** their eyes

    3.  Immediately their eyes received sight

    4.  They followed Him

# The Sermon

The New Testament Scriptures tell of five blind men who received their sight. Only one is known by name, Bartimaeus. He also is identified as the son of Timaeus, which is what his name actually means. Bar = son of; Timaeus = his father. I wonder if it was just a name that latched on to him from friends of the family as they referred to the little blind boy, Timaeus' son = Bar-Timaeus. There certainly was a *stigma* attached to blindness in the Lord's day. Blindness and sight are used in our everyday figurative language.

The world says, "Seeing is believing," but the Lord said, *"Believe and you will see."* The Gospel of John contrasts the two views for us.

The first category is from a worldly view:

John 4:48 – *"Then Jesus said to him, 'Unless you people see signs and wonders, you will by no means believe.'"*

John 6:30 – *"Therefore they said to Him, 'What sign will You perform then, that we may see it and believe You?'"*

John 20:25 – *"The other disciples therefore said to him, 'We have seen the Lord.' But he said to them, 'Unless I see in His hands the print of the nails, and put my finger into the print of the nails, and put my hand into His side, I will not believe.'"*

John 20:27-28 – *"Then He said to Thomas, 'Reach your finger here, and look at My hands; and reach your hand here, and put it into My side. Do not be unbelieving, but believing.' And Thomas answered and said to Him, 'My Lord and my God!'"*

The following category is by the eye of faith:

John 1:50 – *"Jesus answered and said to him (Nathanael), 'Because I said to you, "I saw you under the fig tree," do you believe? You will see greater things than these.'"*

John 3:36 – *"He who believes in the Son has everlasting life; and he who does not believe the Son shall not see life, but the wrath of God abides on him."*

John 11:40 – *"Jesus said to her (Martha), 'Did I not say to you that if you would believe you would see the glory of God?'"*

John 20:29 – *"Jesus said to him, 'Thomas, because you have seen Me, you have believed. Blessed are those who have not seen and yet have believed.'"*

I will never forget my visit to the ophthalmologist. I explained that I had noticed trouble seeing clearly but did not want to make a *spectacle* of myself. She missed the humour but told me to fill out this paperwork and have a seat. Proud of my accomplishment, I delivered my paper work to the receptionist. She said, "Follow me."

As we proceeded down the corridor, I went on to explain my difficulty as if to pry some information from her experience with eye patients. I continued, "It is especially after I have been working on my computer, reading from the monitor, that I have trouble adjusting my sight." She smiled and situated me into the examining chair. In measured tone she spoke to me saying, "Mr. Trogdon, there are various stages through which we all pass." Profound *insight*, I thought, for a receptionist to pass on to a patient.

I waited in the dark until the doctor came in. He asked a few questions as he made his observations. "Hmm," he said. Then, "Uh huh."

"Let me in on it, Doc. Feel free to think out loud, and I'll listen in," I suggested.

He obliged and began, "In our lives, as we mature, we go through various changes, Mr. Trogdon." I thought, he must be related to the receptionist. He continued, "You have a condition."

"I knew it, no doubt caused by my computer monitor. I knew those things could not be good for you…"

"No, Mr. Trogdon, it's not your computer screen," he interrupted, "It's a condition we call, Presbyopia."

"Presbyopia, is that Greek?" I asked.

"No, Latin," he replied.

"Funny, *presbyter* in Greek means elder," I shared.

"Same in Latin," he observed.

"Would I be correct in guessing that *opia* has something to do with eyes?" I questioned.

"You would," he confirmed.

I grimaced as I asked, "Are you saying that my condition is that I have old eyes?" "Mr. Trogdon, we all go through various stages of life," his voice trailing off into the explanation of how I would have to adjust to trifocals. I learned why they call them, *try*-focals, and you don't have to know Greek nor Latin to appreciate the necessary effort.

Jericho is related to vision through the Bible. It was the place near where Moses would **view** the Promised Land from the top of Mount Pisgah before he died (Deut. 32:49). It was there that Joshua sent two spies, not twelve, as Moses had done. Clear to see, is it not? That, if ten out of twelve were bad, next time just send two.

Do you remember the eye problems those ten spies had? They said, *"The land through which we have gone as spies is a land that devours its inhabitants, and all the people whom we saw in it are men of great stature. There we saw the giants (the descendants of Anak came from the giants); and we were like grasshoppers **in our own sight**, and so we were **in their sight**"* (Num. 13:32-33). Talk about a low self-image! Not only that, but we should contrast their "**world-view**" to our perspective on the world and how we see things.

The two spies that Joshua sent were told to, *"Go, view the land, especially Jericho"* (Josh. 2:1). It was at Jericho that the Lord exalted Joshua in the sight of all Israel (Josh. 4:14). It was there that Joshua himself *"lifted his eyes and looked, and behold, a Man stood opposite him with His sword drawn in His hand. And Joshua went to Him and said to Him, 'Are You for us or for our adversaries?' So He said, 'No, but as Commander of the army of the LORD I have now come'"* (Josh. 5:13-14).

Do not let it escape your notice that just as there were two spies sent by Joshua, there evidently were two Jerichos! That is an old Jericho and a new Jericho. It is not unusual even today to have an old city and new city side by side. The Gospel accounts of Mark and Luke report that they were coming into Jericho while Matthew records they were going out. Before you conclude that they did not know if they were coming or going, try to see it from this perspective. Out of the old and into the new, with two blind men, soon to be eyewitnesses, sitting at the gate.

These two blind men saw better than the multitude that was with Him. The crowd told them that "Jesus of Nazareth" was passing by, but they called Him the *"Son of David"* and cried out that He might have mercy on them! The Son of David is Messianic title for the Lord. The relation of the Lord Jesus to David is carried through the Scriptures as the Son, Seed, Offspring, and Root of David. Not only that, but their call for mercy reminds us that through Him we have the sure mercies of David, of which Isaiah prophesied (Isa. 55:3) and Paul preached (Acts 13:34)!

Their view of the Lord Jesus went well beyond the near-sightedness of the Sadducees and the Pharisees! The religious leaders truly were *"the blind leading the blind"* who would not even accept the Lord's diagnosis of their condition saying in denial, *"Are we blind also?"* They thought they could pull the wool over the eyes of another man who was born blind but had received his sight from the Lord. His parents were intimidated by the leaders, but he was not at all blindsided by them when it came to telling it like it is. He, **the sent One**, had washed away his blindness in the pool of Siloam (*"which is translated, **Sent**"*) and had given him 20/20 vision. His testimony was clear, *"One thing I know: that though I was blind, now I see."* He said, *"Why, this is a marvelous thing, that you do not know where He is from; yet He has opened my eyes"* (Jn.9:1-41)!

This makes one want to pray like the psalmist, *"Open my eyes, that I may see wondrous things from Your law"* (Ps. 119:18). When you do, picture how graciously the Lord responded to these blind men. We read that *"Jesus stood still."* Theirs is the only blind faith that was true faith and their blind leap of faith had gotten the attention of the heavenly Man. He called them to Himself and said, *"What do you want Me to do for you?"* What an offer! How would you fill in the blank on this signed cheque in Jesus' name? They did not hesitate, nor did they have to confer with each another. They knew the answer and made their request, *"Lord, that our eyes may be opened."* With heavenly compassion He touched their eyes and they received their sight immediately and they followed Him. They recognized Him by faith before they saw Him by sight.

From Jericho to Jerusalem by way of Bethphage and Bethany probably took them over what is now called Mount Scopus, where there is all kinds of surveillance equipment keeping an eye, if you will, on Jordan, Syria, and the world! We, too, who have looked unto Jesus, have been given a long term view. Paul says that we have been made to *"see what is the fellowship of the mystery, which from the beginning of the ages has been hidden in God who created all things through Jesus Christ"* (Eph. 3:9). Wow, what a sight!

Above all, I notice that Bartimaeus and his friend, upon receiving their sight, followed the Lord. From there, as I mentioned, they made their way up to the Mount of Olives. The next chapter in both Gospel accounts the Lord Jesus sent two of His disciples to fetch a colt for Him to ride into Jerusalem for the so called Triumphal Entry. He would be celebrated that day but crucified five days later! Bartimaeus was a bit late to follow the Lord, or was he? No, it is never too late. You can start right now.

One fanciful thought… Just picture the last person who receives spiritual sight before the Lord Jesus appears to call away His bride, the Church, in the Rapture. Just like Bartimaeus, he will be saved at the last moment, and immediately the Lord will fill all his vision and he will rise to meet the Lord Jesus and follow Him home to heaven to the Father's house! Fanciful? No. It will be a reality for someone. John says it this way, *"It has not yet been revealed what we shall be, but we know that when He is revealed, we shall be like Him, for we shall see Him as He is"* (1 Jn. 3:2).

We live in a world where Satan, *"the god of this age, has **blinded** the minds of those who do not believe, lest the light of the gospel of the glory of Christ, who is the image of God, should shine* *on them"* (2 Cor. 4:4). How does that light shine? It shines through coming into a relationship with the Lord Jesus Christ. The same relationship was experienced by the blind man of John 9 when he was asked, *"'Do you believe in the Son of God?' He answered and said, 'Who is He, Lord, that I may believe in Him?' And Jesus said to him, 'You have both seen Him and it is He who is talking with you.' Then he said, 'Lord, I believe!' And he worshiped Him"* (Jn. 9:35-38).

For us today, we look with our heart and not with our eyes. It is really no different than the five blind men of the New Testament. They saw with the eye of faith. We, too, must exercise faith in Christ. *"For it is the God who commanded light to shine out of darkness, who has shone in our hearts to give the light of the knowledge of the glory of God in the face of Jesus Christ"* (2 Cor. 4:6).

We actually have it better than they. Doubting Thomas helps us to see this. He missed the eye exam on resurrection evening. The other ten disciples saw 20/20! I have a verse for this, you know. I'm sure you *saw* it coming… The spiritual eye exam results are found in John 20:20 - *"Now when He had said this, He showed them His hands and His side. Then the disciples were glad when they saw the Lord."*

However, Thomas said, *"Unless I see … I will not believe"* (Jn. 20:25)! His eyes were opened one week later. Having seen the Lord, he confessed, *"My Lord and My God!"* The Lord then explained, *"Thomas, because you have seen Me, you have believed. Blessed are those who have not seen and yet have believed"* (Jn. 20:28-29). So, it is more blessed to believe in our hearts, based on what the Scriptures say, than to see with our eyes.

The apostle Paul builds on this saying, *"Therefore, from now on, we regard* (Gr. *eido* = to see, perceive) *no one according to the flesh. Even though we have known Christ according to the flesh, yet now we know Him thus no longer"* (2 Cor. 5:16). Seeing Christ by faith through the Word of God clears up the vision problem. Can you see like the blind men, or do you still go by sight?

I have heard of an eye clinic that fits your prescription lenses and then uses a card with a Scripture verse for you to read to prove your improved sight. The verse is John 3:3, *"Most assuredly, I say to you, unless one is born again, he cannot see the kingdom of God."* Next time you have an eye exam and the doctor uses a card and asks if you can see it, if it has this verse on it, the answer is, "Yes and Amen!"

Be Thou my vision, O Lord of my heart
Naught be all else to me, Save that Thou art;
Thou my best thought, By day or by night
Waking or sleeping, Thy presence my light.

### He Touched Me!

# Personal Testimony

He touched me, O He touched me,
And O the joy that floods my soul!
Something happened, and now I know,
He touched me and made me whole.

—Bill Gaither

Having reflected on God's wonderful Word, and the seven times or situations the Lord Jesus touched someone, I thought it would be good to tell you how He touched my life. Since I am using the analogy of touch, I would like to use my hand as an illustration. With its four fingers and one thumb, you must admit, it is a **handy** illustration indeed.

Allow me to point out my first finger. We usually refer to it as the "pointer finger." Growing up I had heard the verse in Romans 3:23, *"For all have sinned and fall short of the glory of God,"* and could even quote it. Ironically, I applied it to everyone else but myself, that is, until I had fallen into the very things which I had identified as sin in other people's lives. For the first time in my life, I realized that the *"all"* in Romans 3:23 included me! To me, it was the finger of God pointing out my sin. I was guilty before God.

My sin and guilt became a terrible burden that I could not get rid of. It bothered me to look into a mirror and come face to face with myself. For a few years I tried to ignore it, hide it, and even deny it, by comparing myself with others who were worse sinners, at least in my estimation. Then I heard that the wages of sin is death, as stated so clearly in Romans 6:23; I knew I was in danger and needed a Saviour.

I was relieved to hear that God had made a provision for me and my sin through His Son, the Lord Jesus Christ. I read Romans 5:8 with wonder, hanging onto each phrase, *"But God demonstrates His own love toward us, in that while we were still sinners, Christ died for us."* It seemed so simple, too simple and too good to be true.

All my life I had thought that when I die, God would weigh my good works against my bad works, and if I had enough good works to qualify for heaven, He would let me in. At that point in my life, I was past thinking my good would outweigh my bad. I was then wondering if God was open to explanations, as if I could plead my own unique case.

But I was hearing a different message, that God loved me already, that Christ died to pay for all my sins, and that I could have eternal life as a free gift, by faith and not by works. I tried to find something in the Bible to contradict this message of grace, but search as I did, I came up with nothing. Every time I heard the gospel message, I would mark the text and go home and read the chapter before and the chapter after, just looking for anything that would support my misconception.

Bible verses that brought me out of my darkness and into His light were Ephesians 2:8-9 which says, *"For by grace you have been saved through faith, and that not of yourselves; it is the gift of God, not of works, lest anyone should boast."* Another was Titus 3:5, *"Not by works of righteousness which we have done, but according to His mercy He saved us."* The verse that left me no wriggle room at all was Romans 11:6 which says, *"And if by grace, then it is no longer of works; otherwise grace is no longer grace. But if it is of works, it is no longer grace; otherwise work is no longer work."*

After three months of searching, I was convinced that eternal life was the gift of God and not bestowed on the basis of works and that any good things I might have done would have only been filthy rags in His sight (Isaiah 64:6). From the things I had heard during this time of searching, I knew that according to Romans 10:9-10 that I must believe in my heart to be saved and *"call upon the name of the Lord"* (Rom. 10:13).

I'll never forget that night, when all alone, I opened my Bible and asked the Lord to show me what to do. I read 2 Corinthians 6:1-2 which says, *"We then, as workers together with Him also plead with you not to receive the grace of God in vain,"* and, *"Behold, now is the accepted time; behold, now is the day of salvation."* I figured if now is the time and today is the day, then if I were to die at that moment, I would be lost forever. I bowed my head and the best I knew how, I put my trust in the Lord Jesus Christ as my Saviour.

No, it was not a mystical, ecstatic experience like I expected, but it was the touch of God pointing me to the One whom John the Baptist declared to be, *"The Lamb of God who takes away the sin of the world"* (John 1:29). I had peace with God through the Lord Jesus Christ and His peace continues to thrill my heart. I rejoice to know that I have trusted in the finished work of Christ on the cross of Calvary.

> Calvary covers it all, my past with its sin and stain,
> My guilt and despair, Jesus took on Him there,
> And Calvary covers it all.
> — Mrs. Walter G. Taylor

Now, take that pointer finger and stand it up straight. It becomes "number one." This was the *first thing*, where it all started for me. This is where it must start for anyone. Have you put your trust in the Lord Jesus Christ? If not, look again at this one finger and realize that He is the One who loves you as you are and died for you to prove it. He is the only One who can save.

To offer only one way of salvation is not narrow-minded thinking; it is the only reasonable way. Had God declared two ways or five ways to be saved, it would be utter confusion! No, He made only one way of salvation so that we cannot make a mistake, and that one way is through His Son, Jesus Christ. The Bible says in 1 John 5:12, *"He who has the Son has life; he who does not have the Son of God does not have life."* You know the expression, "No two ways about it." It's true, so, why not receive Him now as your Saviour? Now is the time and today is the day that you can be saved and sure of it.

Now, let me get back to the things **at hand**. Look at the middle finger. I heard an African preacher give a parable about the fingers of a man's hand having an argument over which finger was the most important. It was hilarious to see him go through all the antics and imagery used as the fingers fought and argued among themselves. That is until the middle finger declared, "Alright, I'm going to settle this matter once and for all! Everyone stand up!" he shouted. With that, the preacher held up his right hand with fingers erect and pointing upward. Then he took his left hand and held it horizontally above his right hand as a referee would do to signal "time out." Thus, he showed clearly that the middle finger was the tallest. It was obvious to all watching, the middle finger was indeed the most important.

That middle finger is an ideal example of what the evangelist should do. He should reach out the furthest. Think of reaching out with the gospel as an extension of God's hand that is stretched out still! In His love God reaches out by His marvelous grace to save sinners like me and you. The Lord Jesus said of Himself that He came *"to seek and to save that which was lost"* (Luke 19:10). At the cross God was reaching down to man in His grace. We respond by reaching up by faith.

I thank God for those evangelists who reached out to me with the touch of God by the gospel. Those who witnessed to me, prayed for me, preached to me, and loved me. It was as the apostle Paul declared in 2 Corinthians 5:20, *"as though God were pleading through us: we implore you on Christ's behalf, be reconciled to God."* It was the Lord's hand extended through His people.

The third finger in my **handy** illustration takes me to the ring finger. It represents a commitment and love that a married couple has for each other. It also reminds me of the love that the Lord Jesus Christ has for His bride, the church. He wants us to have that same love for one another. One of the proofs that we have passed from death to life is a love for the brethren (1 John 3:14).

When the Lord re-commissioned Simon Peter from being a fisher of men to being a shepherd of sheep, His sheep, He asked him three times, "Do you love Me?" In this series of three questions, the Lord used two different words for love. While it is a worthy study to look into, I only want to point out in simplicity that to care for God's sheep and lambs, a shepherd must love the Lord. Yes, he must love the sheep, God's people, too, but ultimately, love for Christ is the motivation of shepherding the flock of God.

Our family has been greatly blessed by the ones that God has brought into our lives who have cared for us as faithful shepherds. Their counsel and correction have proved invaluable in our lives. I could never put a price on the encouragement that they have imparted to us over the years. I am sure they would never put a price on their ministry either. They were obviously motivated by their love for Christ, just as the apostle Paul who wrote in 2 Corinthians 5:14-15, *"For the love of Christ compels us because we judge thus: that if One died for all, then all died; and He died for all, that those who live should live no longer for themselves, but for Him who died for them and rose again."*

Least of all the four fingers is the little finger. I once heard the ministry of teaching the Word of God compared to the little finger not because teaching the Word of God is insignificant, but teaching the Word is like the little finger because the job of the teacher is to get the Word of God into the ears of the people.

I sought the counsel of godly men concerning the study of the Scriptures and was well advised to make the Bible itself my education plan. You see, the Bible has sixty-six classrooms, thirty-five instructors, a prepaid tuition (just add time), a lifetime curriculum, and One Divine Teacher who was given to guide us into all truth.

I began my Christian education the moment I trusted the Lord as my Saviour and started reading my Bible with understanding for the first time because I then knew the Author Himself. I thank God for wonderful Bible-teaching programs through radio ministries available twenty-four hours a day, seven days a week. I listened on my way to work, while I worked on my job, and on the way home. What an increasing array of teachers we have through this media.

The written ministry in books and periodicals are like old friends living in my library which were either given to me along the way or came at a price. Many have traveled to and from Africa on a slow boat in boxes while we flew by a quicker and easier route.

I treasure my time with certain teachers of the Word who have given of themselves to teach me the things they have received from the Lord. They did what Paul wrote to Timothy in his second epistle, *"And the things that you have heard from me among many witnesses, commit these to faithful men who will be able to teach others also"* (2 Tim. 2:2). Their words and their walk have been the best influence on my life over the years. Some are already with the Lord while others are still serving here in the harvest field, but all are very much alive in my heart; their words are as fresh in my ears as my little finger when the need arises.

Believe me when I say that anything I share of value in my ministry has not originated from me but has been placed in my life by others who have given freely for the glory of God. I thank God for those whom He has brought into my life that have sharpened me as iron sharpens iron (Prov. 27:17).

When it comes to this handy illustration, I know you will agree that these four fingers have their place. Now, we must add the thumb to their number to get a grip on the truth.

The grip that we get on the truth assures our hearts that we are secure in Christ. We are safe in the hollow of His hand. Think of our security as the double grip of God. The Lord said in John 10: 28, *"And I give them eternal life, and they shall never perish; neither shall anyone snatch them out of My hand."* Then in John 10:29 He explains saying, *"My Father, who has given them to Me, is greater than all; and no one is able to snatch them out of My Father's hand."* So, we are safe in our Lord's hand, and we are safe in His Father's hand. Finally, in John 10:30 we read, *"I and My Father are one."* We are secure in the grip, the double grip of God's love in Christ. We know that nothing is able to separate us from the love of God which is in Christ Jesus our Lord (Romans 8:38-39). We are saved by what Christ did on the cross and we are sure by what God has written in His Word.

This is how the Lord touched me. I hope that by hearing my story, you will be able to relate to it and see how God can touch your life. He is reaching your way through a *handful* of people.

# He Touched Me!
## Finishing Touches

Does God still touch people today? Yes, of course He does. How? He touches people through you and me. I know it will not be in the exact same way He did then, but we can easily see how His earthly ministry so long ago compares to His heavenly ministry now. Let me **touch** on these very same areas of His ministry that He can do through you.

### *Strength to Serve*

Simon Peter's mother-in-law was weak and had no strength to serve, yet she had all these people coming to dinner. Hospitality is a great ministry. It is one of the spiritual gifts given to the Body of Christ for service and is even a requirement for elders, which I am sure would pertain mostly to the wife of an elder. Peter himself writes to believers to be hospitable to one another and adds that we should do so, *"without grumbling"* (1 Pet. 4:9). It sounds like he had some inside information. *Touché!*

Now, can you think of someone who is working and serving diligently in this area? While we are not to grow weary **of** doing good, we can sometimes become weary **while** doing good. You could be of help to that person and find a way to add just the right **touch** to the meal by offering to prepare a dish or dessert. Perhaps you could offer to use your home to entertain and fill your dinner table with guests. It may be that you are the one who is in need of help. In that case, highlight this paragraph and share it with a friend.

Seriously, don't be **out of touch** with the needs around you. There are many who could use a helping hand, just like Simon Peter's mother-in-law. You can be that touch of God in their lives. Before you are tempted to think that you cannot meet the needs of others, there are two verses you should balance. Jesus said, *"Without Me you can do nothing"* (John 15:5), but the apostle Paul learned the secret of serving and passes on to us the balance needed for service. He wrote, *"I can do all things through Christ who strengthens me"* (Phil. 4:13). So, while it is true that without Him we can do nothing, it is overwhelmingly true that with Him we can do all things.

Still not convinced? If you are concerned about your weaknesses, you are in good company. Paul came to the conclusion to which we must also come to if we are going to be of any use to God. He said, *"I take pleasure in infirmities, in reproaches, in needs, in persecutions, in distresses, for Christ's sake. For when I am weak, then I am strong"* (2 Cor. 12:10). Now is time we say, "Lord, use me to touch others' lives."

## Cleansing the Leper

When the Lord cleansed the leper, he was healed of a dread disease that represents sin and uncleanness. We live in a society with people who are suffering with illness that the world deems as *untouchables*. They are not. They are desperately waiting on the outskirts of life for someone, anyone, who will care enough to make contact. We do not have the power in ourselves to cleanse from disease, but we can put people **in touch** with the Lord who is able to cleanse from every sin and stain.

If the uncleanness is that of sin, they can be forgiven. If it is the sad situation of disease, the Lord has grace which is sufficient for the need. It is a high calling to minister to those who are suffering but what an opportunity to show His mercy and love with the touch of God on their lives.

## Raising the Dead

Death, a cold, veiled stranger to most of us, has an appointment that we all must keep someday. The Lord of life intervened in a wonderful way in raising the widow's son at the village of Nain. He reached out and touched the coffin during the funeral procession. To do so, He came close. His presence was known, and His touch effective. How good to know that our last enemy, death, has been defeated through the resurrection of our Lord. Our sorrow for the loss of a loved one who knew the Lord is not hopeless sorrow but hope-filled. One day we shall see them again (1 Thess. 4:13-18).

When death touches a family, we should make our presence known and be available to help in their time of loss. We read that the Lord saw this woman and had compassion on her. He said little. We should follow our Lord's example. Just your being there for them is often best. It is no time for sermons or plaudits, but it is a time of sharing their grief. This is the best way to minister His touch.

## Healing the Deaf-Mute & Restoring the Servant's Ear

When I read how the Lord opened the ears of the deaf through His touch, I cannot help but think of the communications of the times in which we live. Years ago the telephone company had a jingle, "Reach out and touch someone." We still refer to communications as staying "in touch." In order to stay **in touch** we've gone from telephones to cell phones, from letters to emails, to texting to instant messaging, and from computers to video phones. Whatever your choice of communication, it is still for the purpose of being *in touch*.

The biggest challenge to the communication of the gospel is not that people cannot hear, but that they will not hear. They refuse to listen to the message. We need His touch to help us to first win the right to be heard and then to *"always be ready to give a defense to everyone who asks you a reason for the hope that is in you, with meekness and fear"* (1 Pet. 3:15). When the Lord uses you to open someone's ears, remember to give them His Word. The Bible says, *"Faith comes by hearing and hearing by the Word of God"* (Rom. 10:17). It is only His Word that God has promised to honour. So, when we have the ears of people open, give the real *text message* and "reach out and touch someone" today!

## Calming Fears

The Bible says that in the last days men's hearts will be failing them for fear and the expectation of those things which are coming on the earth. We may not be at the point of heart failure, but people's hearts are already gripped with fear. There are phobias of every kind. There is fear of the unknown, fear of judgement, fear of failure, fear of death, and even fear of fear itself. Not all fear is bad. A surgeon fears infection, and I'm glad to know that when I go to the hospital. We are told in the Bible to fear God, yet the God whom we fear is the One who tells us, *"Do not be afraid."* He delivers us from all our fear (Psalm 34:4).

Someone has said, "God comforts the afflicted and afflicts the comfortable," but we need the comforting ministry of His touch more now than ever before. How can God use us to comfort? First, there is the comfort of the Holy Spirit. He Himself is called, *"the Comforter"* (John 14:16, 26; 15:26; 16:7). He is the One called alongside of us to help us. Secondly, there is the comfort of the Scriptures so that *"we through the patience and **comfort** of the Scriptures might have hope"* (Rom. 15:4). Lastly, we are a comfort, as His saints, through whom *"the God of all comfort, who comforts us in all our tribulation, that we may be able to comfort those who are in any trouble, with the comfort with which we ourselves are comforted by God"* (2 Cor. 1:3-4). In other words, when you go through trials, remember how the Lord comforts you so that when others are going through difficulties, you may be able to comfort them in the same way.

## Let the Little Children Come!

How sad that we live in a society that when it comes to children, mankind has turned touch into something dangerous. The Lord takes any kind of misconduct toward children very seriously. Children are the innocents among us, and that is all the more reason to see to their protection. However, you can still touch their lives in a safe and loving way. Parents have the most opportune way of touching their children for the Lord by raising them in the nurture and admonition of the Lord.

Even if you do not have children of your own, in the family of God we have the privilege of praying for the children around us. Sunday School teachers can impact students' lives for good; youth workers and summer camp workers also add so much to these young ones who grow and mature into men and women for God. Never underestimate the value of a smile. The acceptance of children in your home or local church sends a touching message to their little hearts. Greeting cards for special occasions, addressed to them personally, are very impressive.

## Eyes to See

Finally, opening the eyes of the blind can be easily applied to how the Lord can use you to touch people in your world today.

Remember how our Lord went about doing good and meeting people where they were, people like you and me with a variety of conditions and in a variety of situations. We not only relate to those people of whom we have read about in the Scriptures, but we also come into contact with people like them every day. Just as He was touched with the feeling of our infirmities, we should be touched with the needs all around us.

God still reaches out with His hand through His Son and through us if we are willing to be used by Him to touch someone. You can present yourself to God right now and say, "Lord, please use me to reach out and touch someone today. Give me strength to serve, cleanness of life, a passion for souls, ears to hear, courage to act, childlike faith, and eyes to see. Fill me with your love and compassion so that my touch becomes an extension of your touch. Amen."

# The Beauty of Jesus in Me

My life touched yours for a very brief space
And what, oh what did you see;
A hurried, a worried, an anxious face,
or the beauty of Jesus in me?

Was I steeped so deep in the things of this world
that you couldn't detect one thing;
That would set me apart and show that my heart
belonged to the heavenly King?

Did I carry no banner for Jesus my Lord,
Not one thing at all that could show
Whose side I am on in this glorious fight?
I am His! But you couldn't know.

Forgive me! And if we should ere meet again
Upon earth, oh, I pray you will see
No mark of this world, but His banner unfurled,
And the beauty of Jesus in me!
—Alice Hansche Mortenson

## Prophets Foretold Him
### by Timothy Cross

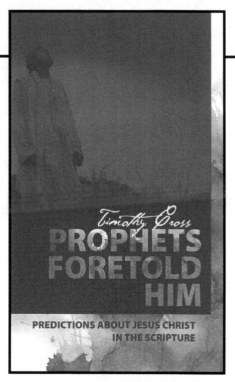

PREDICTIONS ABOUT JESUS CHRIST IN THE SCRIPTURE

The life and ministry of the Lord Jesus did not occur in a vacuum, for Prophets Foretold Him. Jesus said of Himself that *"The Son of Man goes as it is written of Him..."* (Matthew 26:24). With our New Testament hindsight therefore, it is possible to construct a life of Christ from Scriptures written many centuries before He lived and ministered here on earth. In this book, we do just that. Amazingly, here is The Life of Christ BC.

This volume considers some of the many prophecies Almighty God revealed beforehand concerning His Son, and their amazing, detailed and, humanly speaking, inexplicable fulfilment in the fullness of time. Fulfilled prophecy is one of the many evidences that the Bible is no ordinary book but the very Word of the living God. Only the eternal God knows the future, and thus only the eternal God can truly reveal the future.

Be prepared to be amazed! Here is a book to further your confidence in and wonder at the inspired Word of God. And here is a book to fuel your devotion to the One of Whom all Scripture points: the Lord Jesus Christ. The inspired Word and the incarnate Word cannot be separated.

ISBN: 9-781926-765242
US: $9.99
Canada: $11.99
Pages: 100

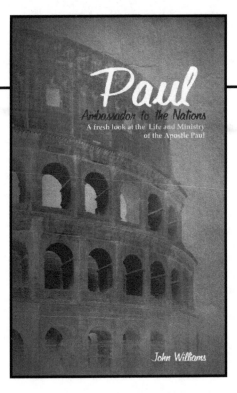

## Paul: Ambassador to the Nations
### by John Williams

## A fresh look at the Life and Ministry of the Apostle Paul

"Another book about the Apostle Paul?"—you may ask. Yes, but one written from a different perspective. This is not a biography, nor is it an outline of Pauline theology. In these chapters we shall see Paul "wearing his many different hats," and functioning in a wide variety of settings. Hopefully, we shall identify with the Apostle, at least to some degree, then seek to follow his noble example. Do you aspire to be a preacher, a teacher, a pastor, an elder, a deacon, a Sunday School helper or youth worker? Do you sense God is calling you to missionary service? Are you gifted as a church planter or a pioneer in some corner of the harvest field? Has God gifted you as a writer or a thinker, someone able to help us understand the great concepts of Scripture and Christian theology? Or, perhaps you see yourself as, "just one of those ordinary members of the Body of Christ," who help make things tick.

However you choose to answer those questions, please be assured that Paul, the bond-slave of Jesus, has something important to say to you.

ISBN: 9-780830-746897
US: $12.99
Canada: $14.99
Pages: 164

## Judges: Book of Heroes
## by Tim Mather

Judges: Book of Heroes traces the tragic story of the people of God from the glory days of Joshua to the gloomy days of Samson; from courage to compromise; from conquest to capitulation. But despite the subject matter, this book is not a gloomy book! The author shows that for all their failings, the judges were men and women of rare faith, men and women who stood for God in troubled times. And he encourages us, too, to live for God where He has placed us; to serve Him faithfully in the work to which He has called us.

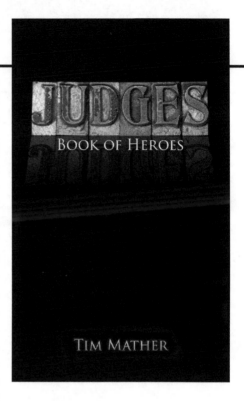

"We may not have the spiritual gifts of a Samson or a Deborah. We may not have the courage of an Othniel or a Jephthah. Perhaps we're just ordinary, like Gideon, or maybe we feel like one of the minor judges, like Abodon or Ibzan or Tola, whose names nobody can remember. Nevertheless, God delights to use ordinary people, and He delights even more to use really useless people! God will use those who have faith in Him, those whose hearts are loyal to Him. The judges of Israel, imperfect as they were, stand out for God like shining beacons in a dark night, because at the end of the day, they trusted God, and were available to Him."

ISBN: 9-781926-765297
US: $14.99
Canada: $17.99
Pages: 236

## Winning Is Everything
### by Tony Hart

With contemporary illustrations, clear Biblical exposition and in the common man's language, Dr. Tony Hart helps us to experientially know what it means to be more than conquerors in Christ and how we can more seriously accept our responsibility to remain faithful to God's Word, while courageously preventing the enemy's plan from governing our lives.

May God richly bless you as you read and apply these practical truths from God's Word.

~from the forward by Dr Tony Evans
Senior Pastor - Oak Cliff Bible Fellowship
President - Urban Alternative

ISBN: 9-781897-117750
US: $9.99
Canada: $10.99
Pages: 128